A Guide To Health

by

Mahatma Gandhi And A. Rama Iyer

Double 9 BOOKS

A Guide To Health

by Mahatma Gandhi And A. Rama Iyer

ISBN: 978-93-59954-71-4

Published by

DOUBLE 9 BOOKS
2/13-B, Ansari Road
Daryaganj, New Delhi – 110002
info@double9books.com
www.double9books.com
Tel. 011-40042856

ABOUT THE AUTHOR

Mohandas Karamchand Gandhi (October 2, 1869 – January 30, 1948) was an Indian lawyer, anti-colonial patriot, and political ethicist who led the successful movement for India's independence from British control through peaceful resistance. He sparked civil rights and freedom movements all across the world. The epithet Mahtm (from Sanskrit for 'great-souled, venerable') was initially ascribed to him in South Africa in 1914 and is now used worldwide. Gandhi, he was brought up in a Hindu family on the Gujarat coast, learned law at the Inner Temple in London, he was called to the bar at the age of 22 in June 1891. He traveled to South Africa in 1893 to represent an Indian merchant in a dispute after two uncertain years in India, when he was unable to establish a successful law practice. He afterwards spent 21 years in South Africa. It was here that Gandhi raised a family and first used nonviolent resistance in a civil rights struggle. In 1915, at the age of 45, he went to India and immediately began organizing peasants, farmers, and urban laborers to protest exorbitant land taxation and discrimination.

CONTENTS

INTRODUCTION

For more than twenty years past I have been paying special attention to the question of Health. While in England, I had to make my own arrangements for food and drink, and I can say, therefore, that my experience is quite reliable. I have arrived at certain definite conclusions from that experience, and I now set them down for the benefit of my readers.

As the familiar saying goes, 'Prevention is better than cure.' It is far easier and safer to prevent illness by the observance of the laws of health than to set about curing the illness which has been brought on by our own ignorance and carelessness. Hence it is the duty of all thoughtful men to understand aright the laws of health, and the object of the following pages is to give an account of these laws. We shall also consider the best methods of cure for some of the most common diseases.

As Milton says, the mind can make a hell of heaven or a heaven of hell. So heaven is not somewhere above the clouds, and hell somewhere underneath the earth! We have this same idea expressed in the Sanskrit saying, *Mana êva Manushayanâm Kâranam Bandha Mokshayoh*—man's captivity or freedom is dependant on the state of his mind. From this it follows that whether a man is healthy or unhealthy depends on himself. Illness is the result not only of our actions but also of our thoughts. As has been said by a famous doctor, more people die for fear of diseases like small-pox, cholera and plague than out of those diseases themselves.

Ignorance is one of the root-causes of disease. Very often we get bewildered at the most ordinary diseases out of sheer ignorance, and in our anxiety to get better, we simply make matters worse. Our ignorance of the most elementary laws of health leads us to adopt wrong remedies or drives us into the hands of the veriest quacks. How strange (and yet how true) it is that we know much less about things near at hand than things at a distance. We know hardly anything of our own village, but we can give by rote the names of the rivers and mountains of England! We take so much trouble to learn the names of the stars in the sky, while we hardly think it worth while to know the things that are in our own homes! We never care a jot for the splendid pageantry of Nature before our very eyes, while we are so anxious to witness the puerile mummeries of the theatre! And in the same way, we are not ashamed to be ignorant of the structure of our body, of the way in which the bones and muscles, grow, how the blood circulates and is rendered impure, how we are affected by evil thoughts and passions, how our mind travels over illimitable spaces and times while the body is at rest, and so on. There is nothing so closely connected with us as our body, but there is also nothing perhaps of which our ignorance is so profound, or our indifference so complete.

It is the duty of every one of us to get over this indifference. Everyone should regard it as his bounden duty to know something of the fundamental facts concerning his body. This kind of instruction should indeed be made compulsory in our schools. At present, we know not how to deal with the most ordinary scalds and wounds; we are helpless if a thorn runs into our foot; we are beside ourselves with fright and dismay if we are bitten by an ordinary snake! Indeed, if we consider the depth of our ignorance in such matters, we shall have to hang down our heads in shame. To assert that the average man cannot be expected to know these things is simply absurd. The following pages are intended for such as are willing to learn.

I do not pretend that the facts mentioned by me have not been said before. But my readers will find here in a nutshell the substance of several books on the subject. I have arrived at my conclusions after studying these books, and after a series of careful experiments. Moreover, those who are new to this subject will also be saved the risk of being confounded by the conflicting views held by writers of such books. One writer says for instance, that hot water is to be used under certain circumstances, while another writer says that, exactly under the same circumstances, cold water is to be used. Conflicting views of this kind have been carefully considered by me, so that my readers may rest assured of the reliability of my own views.

We have got into the habit of calling in a doctor for the most trivial diseases. Where there is no regular doctor available, we take the advice of mere quacks. We labour under the fatal delusion that no disease can be cured without medicine. This has been responsible for more mischief to mankind than any other evil. It is of course, necessary that our diseases should be cured, but they cannot be cured *by medicines*. Not only are medicines merely useless, but at times even positively harmful. For a diseased man to take drugs and medicines would be as foolish as to try to cover up the filth that has accumulated in the inside of the house. The more we cover up the filth, the more rapidly does putrefaction go on. The same is the case with the human body. Illness or disease is only Nature's warning that filth has accumulated in some portion or other of the body; and it would surely be the part of wisdom to allow Nature to remove the filth, instead of covering it up by the help of medicines. Those who take medicines are really rendering the task of Nature doubly difficult. It is, on the other hand, quite easy for us to help Nature in her task by remembering certain elementary principles,—by fasting, for instance, so that the filth may not accumulate all the more, and by vigorous exercise in the open air, so that some of the filth may escape in the form of perspiration. And the one thing that is supremely necessary is to keep our minds strictly under control.

We find from experience that, when once a bottle of medicine gets itself introduced into a home, it never thinks of going out, but only goes on drawing other bottles in its train. We come across numberless human beings who are afflicted by some disease or other all through their lives in spite of their pathetic devotion to medicines. They are to-day under the treatment of this doctor, to-morrow of that. They spend all their life in a futile search after a doctor who will cure them for good. As the late Justice Stephen (who was for some time in India) said, it is really astonishing that drugs of which so little is known should be applied by doctors to bodies of which they know still less! Some of the greatest doctors of the West themselves have now come to hold this view. Sir Astley Cooper, for instance, admits that the 'science' of medicine is mostly mere guess-work; Dr. Baker and Dr. Frank hold that more people die of medicines than of diseases; and Dr. Masongood even goes to the extent of saying that more men have fallen victims to medicine than to war, famine and pestilence combined!

It is also a matter of experience that diseases increase in proportion to the increase in the number of doctors in a place. The demand for drugs has become so widespread that even the meanest papers are sure of getting advertisements of quack medicines, if of nothing else. In a recent book on the Patent Medicines we are told that the Fruit-salts and syrups, for which we pay from Rs. 2 to Rs. 5, cost to their manufacturers only from a quarter of an anna to one anna! No wonder, then, that their compositions should be so scrupulously kept a secret.

We will, therefore, assure our readers that there is absolutely no necessity for them to seek the aid of doctors. To those, however, who may not be willing to boycott doctors and medicines altogether, we will say, "As far as possible, possess your souls in patience, and do not trouble the doctors. In case you are forced at length to call in the aid of a doctor, be sure to get a good man; then, follow his directions strictly, and do not call in another doctor, unless by his own advice. But remember, above all, that the curing of your disease does not rest ultimately in the hands of any doctor."

M. K. Gandhi.

CHAPTER I
THE MEANING OF HEALTH

Ordinarily that man is considered healthy who eats well and moves about, and does not resort to a doctor. But a little thought will convince us that this idea is wrong. There are many cases of men being diseased, in spite of their eating well and freely moving about. They are under the delusion that they are healthy, simply because they are too indifferent to *think* about the matter.

In fact, perfectly healthy men hardly exist anywhere over this wide world.

As has been well said, only that man can be said to be really healthy, who has a sound mind in a sound body. The relation between the body and the mind is so intimate that, if either of them got out of order, the whole system would suffer. Let us take the analogy of the rose-flower. Its colour stands to its fragrance in the same way as the body to the mind or the soul. No one regards an artificial paper-flower as a sufficient substitute for the natural flower, for the obvious reason that the fragrance, which forms the essence of the flower, cannot be reproduced. So too, we instinctively honour the man of a pure mind and a noble character in preference to the man who is merely physically strong. Of course, the body and the soul are both essential, but the latter is far more important than the former. No man whose character is not pure can be said to be really healthy. The body which contains a diseased mind can never be anything but diseased. Hence it follows that a pure character is the foundation of health in the real sense of the term; and we may say that all evil thoughts and evil passions are but different forms of disease.

Thus considered, we may conclude that that man alone is perfectly healthy whose body is well formed, whose teeth as well as eyes and ears are in good condition, whose nose is free from dirty matter, whose skin exudes perspiration freely and without any bad smell, whose mouth is also free from bad smells, whose hands and legs perform their duty properly, who is neither too fat nor too thin, and whose mind and senses are constantly under his control. As has already been said, it is very hard to gain such health, but it is harder still to retain it, when once it has been acquired. The chief reason why we are not truly healthy is that our parents were not. An eminent writer has said that, if the parents are *in perfectly good condition* their children would certainly be superior to them in all respects. A *perfectly healthy* man has no reason to fear death; our terrible fear of death shows that we are far from being so healthy. It is, however, the clear duty of all of us to strive for perfect health. We will, therefore, proceed to consider in the following pages how such health can be attained, and how, when once attained, it can also be retained for ever.

CHAPTER II
THE HUMAN BODY

The world is compounded of the five elements,—earth, water, air, fire, and ether. So too is our body. It is a sort of miniature world. Hence the body stands in need of all the elements in due proportion,—pure earth, pure water, pure fire or sunlight, pure air, and open space. When any one of these falls short of its due proportion, illness is caused in the body.

The body is made up of skin and bone, as well as flesh and blood. The bones constitute the frame-work of the body; but for them we could not stand erect and move about. They protect the softer parts of the body. Thus the skull gives protection to the brain, while the ribs protect the heart and the lungs. Doctors have counted 238 bones in the human body. The outside of the bones is hard, but the inside is soft and hollow. Where there is a joint between two bones, there is a coating of marrow, which may be regarded as a soft bone. The teeth, too, are to be counted among the bones.

When we feel the flesh at some points, we find it to be tough and elastic. This part of the flesh is known as the muscle. It is the muscles that enable us to fold and unfold our arms, to move our jaws, and to close our eyes. It is by means of the muscles, again, that our organs of perception do their work.

It is beyond the province of this book to give a detailed account of the structure of the body; nor has the present writer enough knowledge to give such an account. We will, therefore, content ourselves with just as much information as is essential for our present purpose.

The most important portion of the body is the stomach. If the stomach ceases to work even for a single moment, the whole body would collapse. The work of the stomach is to digest the food, and so to provide nourishment to the body. Its relation to the body is the same as that of the steam engine to the Railway train. The gastric juice which is produced in the stomach helps the assimilation of nutritious elements in the food, the refuse being sent out by way of the intestines in the form of urine and fæces. On the left side of the abdominal cavity is the spleen, while to the right of the stomach is the liver, whose function is the purification of the blood and the secretion of the bile, which is so useful for digestion.

In the hollow space enclosed by the ribs are situated the heart and the lungs. The heart is between the two lungs, but more to the left than the right. There are on the whole 24 bones in the chest; the action of the heart can be felt between the fifth and the sixth rib. The lungs are connected with the windpipe. The air which we inhale is taken into the lungs through the windpipe, and the blood is purified by it. It is of the utmost importance to breathe through the nose, instead of through the mouth.

On the circulation of the blood depend all activities of the body. It is the blood that provides nourishment to the body. It extracts the nutritious elements out of the food, and ejects the refuse through the intestines, and so keeps the body warm. The blood is incessantly circulating all over the body, along the veins and the arteries. The beatings of the pulse are due to the circulation of the blood. The pulse of a normal adult man beats some 75 times a minute. The pulses of children beat faster, while those of old men are slower.

The chief agency for keeping the blood pure is the air. When the blood returns to the lungs after one complete round over the body, it is impure and contains poisonous elements. The oxygen of the air which we inhale purifies this blood and is assimilated into it, while the nitrogen absorbs the poisonous matter and is breathed out. This process goes on incessantly. As the air has a very important function to perform in the body, we shall devote a separate chapter to a detailed consideration of the same.

CHAPTER III
AIR

Of the three things that are indispensable for the subsistence of man,—namely, air, water, and food—the first is the most important. Hence it is that God has created it in such large quantities as to make it available to all of us for nothing. Modern civilisation, however, has rendered even fresh air somewhat costly, for, in order to breathe fresh air, we have to go out of towns, and this means expense. The residents of Bombay, for instance, distinctly improve in health in the air of Matheran or, still better, of the Malabar Hills; but they cannot go to these places without money. Hence, in these days, it would be hardly true to say that we get fresh air *gratis,* as we used to in the old days.

But, whether fresh air is available *gratis* or not, it is undeniable that we cannot get on without it. We have already seen that the blood circulates over the body, returns to the lungs, and after being purified, starts on its round again. We breathe out the impure air, and take in oxygen from the outside, which purifies the blood. This process of inspiration and expiration goes on for ever, and on it depends man's life. When drowned in water we die, because, then we are unable to let out the impure air in the body and take in pure air from outside. The divers go down into the water in what is known as a diving bell, and they take in fresh air through a tube which leads to the top. Hence it is that they are able to remain under water for a long time.

It has been ascertained by experiments that no man can live without air for as long as five minutes. We often hear of the death of little children, when they are held so close to the bosom by ignorant mothers as to make it impossible for them to breathe.

We should all be as much against the breathing of impure air as we are against the drinking of dirty water and the eating of dirty food; but the air we breathe is, as a rule, far more impure than the water we drink or the food we eat. We are all worshippers of concrete objects; those things that can be seen and felt are regarded by us as of far greater importance than those which are invisible and intangible. Since air belongs to this latter class of objects, we fail to realise the evil wrought by the impure air that we breathe. We would think twice before eating the leavings of another man's food, or drinking out of a cup polluted by another man's lips. Even those who have not the least sense of shame or repugnance would never eat another man's vomit, or drink the water which has been spat out by him; even those who are dying of hunger and thirst would refuse to do it. But, alas, how few of us realise that the air we inhale is so often the impure and poisonous air which has been exhaled by others, and which is surely no less objectionable than a man's vomit! How strange that men should sit and sleep together for hours in closed rooms, and go on inhaling the deadly air exhaled by themselves and their companions! How fortunate for man that air should be so light and diffusive, and capable of penetrating the smallest holes! Even when the doors and windows are closed, there is generally some little space between the walls and the roof, through which some air from outside manages to get in, so that the inmates of the room have not to breathe exclusively poisoned air. The air that we exhale mixes with the air outside, and is rendered pure again by an automatic process that is always going on in Nature.

Now we are able to understand why so many men and women should be weak and diseased. *There can be absolutely no doubt that impure air is the root-cause of disease in ninety-nine cases out of every hundred.* It follows that the best way of avoiding disease is to live and work in the open air. No doctor can compete with fresh air in this matter. Consumption is caused by the decay of the lungs, due to the inhaling of impure air, just as a steam engine which is filled with bad coal gets out of order. Hence doctors say that the easiest and the most effective treatment for a consumptive patient is to keep him in fresh air for all the 24 hours of the day.

It is, of course, essential to know how we can keep the air pure. In fact, every child should be taught the value of fresh air, as soon as it is able to understand anything. If my readers would take the trouble to learn the simple facts about the air and would put their knowledge into practice, while teaching their children also to do the same. I shall feel immensely gratified.

Our latrines are perhaps most responsible for rendering the air impure. Very few people realise the serious harm done by dirty latrines. Even dogs and cats make with their claws something like a pit wherein to deposit their fæces, and then cover it up with some earth. Where there are no lavatories of the modern approved types, we should also do likewise. There should be kept ashes or dry earth in a tin can or an earthen vessel inside the latrine, and whoever goes into the latrine should, on coming out, cover the fæces well with the ash or the earth, as the case may be. If this is done there would be no bad smell, and the flies too will not settle on it and transmit the filth. Anybody whose sense of smell has not been wholly blunted, or who has not grown thoroughly accustomed to foul smells will know how noxious is the smell that emanates from all filthy matter which is allowed to lie open to the weather. Our gorge rises at the very thought of fæces being mixed with our food, but we go on inhaling the air which has been polluted by such foul smell, forgetting the fact that the one is just as bad as the other, except that, while the former is visible, the latter is not. We should see that our latrines are kept thoroughly neat and clean. We abhor the idea of our cleaning the latrines ourselves, but what we should really abhor is the idea of making use of dirty latrines. What is the harm in ourselves removing the filth which has been expelled from inside our own body, and which we are not ashamed to have removed by others? There is absolutely no reason why we should not ourselves learn the work of scavenging and teach it to our children as well. The filthy matter should be removed, and thrown into a pit two feet deep, and then covered up with a thick layer of earth. If we go to some open place, we should dig a small pit with our hands or feet, and then cover it up, after the bowels have been evacuated.

We also make the air impure by making water at all places indiscriminately. This dirty habit should be given up altogether. If there is no place specially set apart for the purpose, we should go to some dry ground away from the house, and should also cover up the urine with earth.

The filth should not be cast into very deep pits, for, in that case, it would be beyond the reach of sun's heat, and would also pollute the water flowing underneath the earth.

The habit of spitting indiscriminately on the verandahs, court yards, and such like places is also very bad. The spittle, especially of consumptives, is very dangerous. The poisonous germs in it rise into the air, and, being inhaled by others, lead to a spread of the disease. We should keep a spittoon inside the house, and if we have to spit when out on the road we should spit where there is dry dust, so that the spittle may be absorbed into the dust and cause no harm. Doctors hold that the consumptive should spit into a spittoon with some disinfectant in it: for, even if he spits on dry ground, the germs in his spittle manage to rise and spread into the air along with the dust. But, in any case, there can be no doubt that the habit of spitting wherever we please is dirty as well as dangerous.

Some people throw where they like cooked food and other articles, which decay and render the air impure. If all such rubbish be put underground, the air would not be made impure, and good manure, too could be obtained. In fact, no kind of decaying matter should be allowed to lie exposed to the air. It is so easy for us to take this necessary precaution, if only we are in earnest about it.

Now we have seen how our own bad habits render the air impure, and what we can do to keep it pure. Next we shall consider how to inhale the air.

As already mentioned in the last chapter, the air is to be inhaled through the nose, and not through the mouth. There are, however, very few persons who know how to breathe correctly. Many people are in the pernicious habit of inhaling through the mouth. If very cold air is inhaled through the mouth, we catch cold and sore throat. Further, if we inhale through the mouth, the particles of dust in the air go into the lungs and cause great mischief. In London, for instance, in November, the smoke which issues from the chimneys of great factories mixes with the dense fog, producing a kind of yellow mixture. This contains tiny particles of soot, which can be detected in the spittle of a man who inhales through the mouth. To escape this, many women (who have not learnt to breathe through the nose alone) put on a special kind of veil over their faces, which act as sieves. If these veils are closely examined, particles of dust can be detected in them. But God has given to all of us a sieve of this kind inside the nose. The air which is inhaled through the nostrils is sifted before it reaches the lungs, and is also warmed in the process. So all men should learn to breathe through the nose alone. And this is not at all difficult, if we remember to keep our mouth firmly shut at all times, except when we are talking. Those who have got into the habit of keeping their mouth open should sleep with a bandage round the mouth, which would force them to breathe through the nose. They should also take some twenty long respirations in the open air, both in the morning and in the evening. In fact, all men can practise this simple exercise and see for themselves how rapidly their chest deepens. If the chest be measured at the beginning of the practice, and again after an interval of two months, it will be seen how much it has expanded in this short period.

After learning how to inhale the air, we should cultivate the habit of breathing fresh air, day in and day out. We are generally in the most pernicious habit of keeping confined to the house or the office throughout the day, and sleeping in narrow rooms at night, with all doors and windows shut. As far as possible, we should remain in the open air at all times. We should at least *sleep* on the verandah or in the open air. Those who cannot do this should at least keep the doors and windows of the room fully open at all times. The air is our food for all the twenty-four hours of the day. Why, then, should we be afraid of it? It is a most foolish idea that we catch cold by inhaling the cool breeze of the morning. Of course, those people who have spoiled their lungs by the evil habit of sleeping within closed doors are likely to catch cold, if they change their habit all on a sudden. But even they should not be afraid of cold, for this cold can be speedily got rid of. Now-a-days, in Europe, the houses for consumptives are being built in such a way that they may get fresh air at all times. We know what terrible havoc is wrought in India by epidemics. We should remember that these epidemics are due to our habit of defiling the air, and of inhaling this poisonous air. We should understand that even the most delicate people will be benefitted by systematically inhaling fresh air. If we cultivate the habit of keeping the air pure and of breathing only fresh air, we can save ourselves from many a terrible disease.

Sleeping with the face uncovered is as essential as sleeping in fresh air. Many of our people are in the habit of sleeping with the face covered, which means that they have to inhale the poisonous air which has been exhaled by themselves. Fortunately however, some of the air from outside does find its way through the interstices of the cloth, else they should die of suffocation. But the small quantity of air that gains entrance in this way is altogether inadequate. If we are suffering from cold, we may cover the head with a piece of cloth, or put on a night-cap, but the nose should be kept exposed *under all circumstances*.

Air and light are so intimately connected with each other that it is as well to speak a few words here on the value of light. Light is as indispensable to life as air itself. Hence it is that Hell is represented as completely dark. Where light cannot penetrate, the air can never be pure. If we enter a dark cellar, we can distinctly perceive the smell of the foul air. The fact that we cannot see in the dark shows that God has intended us to live and move in the light. And Nature has given us just as much darkness as we require in the night. Yet, many people are in the habit of sitting or sleeping in underground cellars, devoid of air and light, even in the hottest summer! Those who thus deprive themselves of air and light are always weak and haggard.

Now-a-days, there are many doctors in Europe who cure their patients by means of air-bath and sun-bath alone. Thousands of diseased persons have been cured by mere exposure to the air and to the sunlight. We should keep all doors and windows in our houses always open, in order to allow the free entrance of air and light.

Some readers may ask why, if air and light are so indispensable, those who live and work in cellars are not visibly affected. Those who have thought well over the matter would never put this question. Our aim should be to attain the maximum of health by all legitimate means; *we should not be content merely to live anyhow*. It has been indubitably established that insufficient air and light give rise to disease. Dwellers in towns are, as a rule, more delicate than those in the country, for they get less air and light than the latter. Air and light, then, are absolutely indispensable to health, and every one should remember all that we have said on the matter, and act up to it to the best of his ability.

CHAPTER IV
WATER

As has been already pointed out, air is the most indispensable to our subsistence, while water comes next in order. Man cannot live for more than a few minutes without air, but he can live for a few days without water. And in the absence of other food, he can subsist on water alone for many days. There is more than 70% of water in the composition of our food-stuffs, as in that of the human body.

Even though water is so indispensable, we take hardly any pains to keep it pure. Epidemics are as much the outcome of our indifference to the quality of the water we drink, as of the air we breathe. The drinking of dirty water very often produces also the disease of the stone.

Water may be impure in either of two ways,—by issuing from dirty places, or by being defiled by us. Where the water issues from dirty places, we should not drink it at all; nor do we generally drink it. But we do not shrink from drinking the water which has been defiled by ourselves. River-water, for instance, is regarded as quite good for drinking, although we throw into it all sorts of rubbish, and also use it for washing purposes. We should make it a rule never to drink the water in which people bathe. The upper portion of a river should be set apart for drinking water, the lower being reserved for bathing and washing purposes. Where there is no such arrangement, it is a good practice to dig in the sand, and take drinking water therefrom. This water is very pure, since it has been filtered by passage through the sand. It is generally risky to drink well-water, for unless it is well protected, the dirty water at the top would trickle down into the well, and render the water impure. Further, birds and insects often fall into the water and die; sometimes birds build their nests inside the wells; and the dirt from the feet of those who draw water from the well is also washed down into the water. For all these reasons, we should be particularly careful in drinking well-water. Water kept in tubs is also very often impure. If it should be pure, the tubs should be washed clean at frequent intervals, and should be kept covered; we should also see that the tank or well from which the water is taken is kept in good condition. Very few people, however, take such precautions to keep the water pure. Hence the best way of removing the impurities of the water is to boil it well, and, after cooling it, filter it carefully into another vessel through a thick and clean piece of cloth. Our duty, however, does not end with this. We should realise that we owe a duty to our fellowmen in this matter. We should see to it that we do absolutely nothing to defile the water which is used for drinking by the public. We should scrupulously refrain from bathing or washing in the water which is reserved for drinking; we should never answer the calls of nature near the banks of a river, nor cremate the dead bodies there and throw the ashes after cremation into the water.

In spite of all the care that we may take, we find it so difficult to keep water perfectly pure. It may have, for instance, salt dissolved in it, or bits of grass and other decaying matter. Rain water is, of course, the purest, but, before it reaches us, it generally becomes impure by the absorption of the floating matter in the atmosphere. Perfectly pure water has a most beneficial effect on the system; hence doctors administer distilled water to their patients. Those who are suffering from constipation are appreciably benefitted by the use of distilled water.

Many people do not know that water is of two kinds, *soft* and *hard*. Hard water is water in which some kind of salt has been dissolved. Hence, soap does not readily lather in it, and food cannot be easily boiled in it. Its taste is brackish, while soft water tastes sweet. It is much safer to drink soft water, although some people hold that hard water is better by virtue of the presence of nutritious matter dissolved therein. Rain water is the best kind of soft water, and is therefore, the best for drinking purposes. Hard water, if boiled and kept over the fire for some half an hour, is rendered soft. Then it may be filtered and drunk.

The question is often asked, "When should one drink water, and how much?" The only safe answer to this is this: one should drink water only when one feels thirsty, and even then only just enough to quench the thirst. There is no harm in drinking water during the meals or immediately afterwards. Of course, we should not wash the food down with water. If the food refuses to go down of itself, it means that either it has not been well prepared or the stomach is not in need of it.

Ordinarily, there is no need to drink water; and indeed, there *should* be none. As already mentioned, there is a large percentage of water in our ordinary articles of food, and we also add water in cooking them. Why then should we feel thirsty? Those people whose diet is free from such articles as chillies and onions which create an artificial thirst, have rarely any need to drink water. Those who feel unaccountably thirsty must be suffering from some disease or other.

We may be tempted to drink any kind of water that we come across, simply because we see some people doing it with impunity. The reply to this has already been given in connection with air. Our blood has in itself the power of destroying many of the poisonous elements that enter into it, but it has to be renewed and purified, just as the sharp edge of a sword has to be mended when it has been once employed in action. Hence, if we go on drinking impure water, we should not be surprised to find our blood thoroughly poisoned in the end.

CHAPTER V
FOOD

It is impossible to lay down hard and fast rules in the matter of food. What sort of food should we eat, how much of it should be eaten, and at what times,—these are questions on which doctors differ a great deal. The ways of men are so diverse, that the very same food shows different effects on different individuals.

Although, however, it is impossible to say conclusively what sort of food we should eat, it is the clear duty of every individual to bestow serious thought on the matter. Needless to say, the body cannot subsist without food. We undergo all sorts of sufferings and privations for the sake of food. But, at the same time, it is indisputable that 99.9% of men and women in the world eat merely to please the palate. They never pause to think of the after-effects at the time of eating. Many people take purgatives and digestive pills or powders in order to be able to eat thoroughly well. Then there are some people who, after eating to the utmost of their capacity, vomit out all that they have eaten, and proceed to eat the same stuffs once more! Some people, indeed, eat so sumptuously that, for two or three days together, they do not feel hungry at all. In some cases, men have even been known to have died of over-eating. I say all this from my own experience. When I think of my old days, I am tempted to laugh at many things, and cannot help being ashamed of some things. In those days I used to have tea in the morning, breakfast two or three hours afterwards, dinner at one o'clock, tea again at 3 p.m., and supper between 6 and 7! My condition at that time was most pitiable. There was a great deal of superfluous fat on my body, and bottles of medicine were always at hand. In order to be able to eat well, I used to take purgatives very often, as well as some tonic or other. In those days, I had not a *third* of my present capacity for work, in spite of the fact that I was then in the prime of youth. Such a life is surely pitiable, and if we consider the matter seriously, we must also admit it to be mean, sinful and thoroughly contemptible.

Man is not born to eat, nor should he live to eat. His true function is to know and serve his Maker; but, since the body is essential to this service, we have perforce to eat. Even atheists will admit that we should eat merely to preserve our health, and not more than is needed for this purpose.

Turn to the birds and beasts, and what do you find? They never eat merely to please the palate, they never go on eating till their inside is full to overflowing. On the other hand, they eat only to appease their hunger, and even then only just as much as will appease their hunger. They take the food provided by Nature, and do not cook their food. Can it be that man alone is created to worship the palate? Can it be that he alone is destined to be eternally suffering from disease? Those animals that live a natural life of freedom never once die of hunger. Among them there are no distinctions of rich and poor,—of those who eat many times a day, and those who do not get even one meal in the day. These abnormalities are found only among us human beings,—and yet we regard ourselves as superior to the animal creation! Surely those who spend their days in the worship of their stomach are worse than the birds and beasts.

A calm reflection will show that all sins like lying, cheating and stealing are ultimately due to our subjection to the palate. He who is able to control the palate, will easily be able to control the other senses. If we tell lies, or commit theft or adultery, we are looked down upon by society, but, strangely enough, no odium attaches to those who slavishly pander to the palate! It would seem as though this were not a question of morality at all! The fact is that even the best of us are slaves to the palate. No one has yet adequately emphasised the numberless evils that arise from our habit of pandering to the palate. All civilised people would boycott the company of liars, thieves, and adulterers; but they go on eating beyond all limits, and never regard it as a sin at all. Pandering to the palate is not regarded by us as a sin, since all of us are guilty of it, just as dacoity is not regarded as a crime in a village of dacoits; but what is worse, we pride ourselves on it! On occasions of marriage and other festivities, we regard it as a sacred duty to worship the palate; even in times of funeral, we are not ashamed of doing it. Has a guest come? We must gorge him with sweetmeats. If, from time to time, we do not give feasts to our friends and relations, or do not partake of the feasts given by them, we must become objects of contempt. If, having invited our friends to eat with us, we fail to cram them with rich stuffs, we must be regarded as miserly. On holidays, of course, we must have specially rich food prepared! Indeed, what is really a great sin has come to be looked upon as a sign of wisdom! We have sedulously cultivated such false notions in the matter of eating that we never realise our slavishness and our beastliness. How can we save ourselves from this terrible state?

Let us view the question from another standpoint. We find it invariably the case in the world that Nature herself has provided for all creatures, whether man or beast, or bird or insect, just enough food for their sustenance. This is an eternal law of Nature. In the kingdom of Nature, none goes to sleep, none forgets to do his duty, and none shows a tendency to laziness. All the work is done to perfection, and punctually to the minute. If we remember to order our lives strictly in accordance with the immutable and eternal laws of Nature, we shall find that there are no more deaths by starvation anywhere over the wide world. Since Nature always provides just enough food to feed all created beings, it follows that he who takes to himself more than his normal share of food, is depriving another of his legitimate share. Is it not a fact, that, in the kitchens of emperors and kings, of all rich men, in general, much more food is prepared than is required to feed them and all their dependents? That is to say, they snatch so much food from the share of the poor. Is it, then, any wonder that the poor should die of starvation? If this is true (and this fact has been admitted by the most thoughtful men) it must necessarily follow that all the food that we eat beyond our immediate need is food filched from the stomachs of the poor. And to the extent to which we eat merely with a view to pleasing the palate must our health necessarily suffer. After this preliminary discussion, we can proceed to consider what kind of food is best for us.

Before, however, we decide the question of the ideal food for us, we have to consider what kinds of food are injurious to health, and to be avoided. Under the term "food", we include all the things that are taken into the body through the mouth,—including *wine, bhang* and *opium, tobacco, tea, coffee and cocoa, spices* and *condiments*. I am convinced that all these articles have to be completely eschewed, having been led to this conviction partly from my own experience, and partly from the experiences of others.

Wine, bhang and opium have been condemned by all the religions of the world, although the number of total abstainers is so limited. Drink has brought about the ruin of whole families. The drunkard forfeits his sanity; he has even been known to forget the distinction between mother, wife and daughter. His life becomes a mere burden to him. Even men of sound sense become helpless automatons when they take to drink; even when not actually under its influence, their minds are too impotent to do any work. Some people say that wine is harmless when used as medicine, but even European doctors have begun to give up this view in many cases. Some partisans of drink argue that, if wine can be used as medicine with impunity, it can also be used as drink. But many poisons are employed as medicines; do we ever dream of employing them as food? It is quite possible that, in some diseases, wine may do some good, but even then, no sensible, or thoughtful man should consent to use it *even as medicine*, under any circumstances. As for opium, it is no less injurious than wine, and is to be equally eschewed. Have we not seen a mighty nation like the Chinese falling under the deadly spell of opium, and rendering itself incapable of maintaining its independence?

Have we not seen the *jagirdars* of our own land forfeiting their *jagirs* under the same fatal influence?

So powerful is the spell that has been woven over the minds of men by tobacco that it will take an age to break it. Young and old have equally come under this fatal spell. Even the best men do not shrink from the use of tobacco. Its use, indeed, has become a matter of course with us, and is spreading wider and wider every day. Very few people are aware of the many tricks employed by the cigarette-manufacturers to bring us more and more under its influence. They sprinkle opium or some perfumed acid on the tobacco, so that we may find it all the more difficult to extricate ourselves from its clutches. They spend thousands of pounds in advertisements. Many European firms dealing in cigars keep their own presses, have their own cinemas, institute lotteries, and give away prizes, and, in short, spend money like water to achieve their end. Even women have now begun to smoke. And poems have been composed on tobacco, extolling it as the great friend of the poor!

The evils of smoking are too numerous to mention. The habitual smoker becomes such a bond slave to it that he knows no sense of shame or compunction; he proceeds to emit the foul fumes even in the houses of strangers! It is also a matter of common experience that smokers are often tempted to commit all sorts of crimes. Children steal money from their parents' purses; and even the prisoners in gaols manage to steal cigarettes and keep them carefully concealed. The smoker will get on without food, but he cannot dispense with his smoke! Soldiers on the field of battle have been known to lose all capacity for fighting for failure of the indispensable cigarette at the critical moment.

The late Count Leo Tolstoi of Russia tells us the following story. A certain man once took it into his head, for some reason, to murder his wife. He actually drew the knife and was about to do the deed, when he felt some compunction, and gave it up. Then he sat down to smoke and his wits being turned under the influence of tobacco, he rose once more and actually committed the murder. Tolstoi held the view that the poison of tobacco is more subtle and irresistible, and hence far more dangerous, than that of wine.

Then the money that is spent on cigars and cigarettes by individuals is frightfully large. I have myself come across instances of cigars consuming as much as Rs. 75 a month for one man!

Smoking also leads to an appreciable reduction of digestive powers. The smoker feels no appetite for food, and in order to give it some flavour, spices and condiments have to be freely used. His breath stinks, and, in some cases, blisters are formed on his face, and the gums and teeth turn black in colour. Many also fall a prey to terrible diseases. The fumes of tobacco befoul the air around, and public health suffers in consequence. I cannot understand how those who condemn drink can have the temerity to defend smoking. The man who does not eschew tobacco in all its forms can never be perfectly healthy, nor can he be a man of pure and blameless character.

I must say that tea, coffee and cocoa are equally injurious to health, although I know that very few are likely to agree with me. There is a kind of poison in all of them; and, in the case of tea and coffee, if milk and sugar were not added, there would be absolutely no nutritious element in them. By means of repeated and varied experiments it has been established that there is nothing at all in these articles which is capable of improving the blood. Until a few years ago, we used to drink tea and coffee only on special occasions, but to-day they have become universally indispensable. Things have come to such a pass that even sickly persons often use them as substitutes for nourishing food!

Fortunately for us, the costliness of cocoa has prevented its spread to the same extent as tea and coffee, although, in the homes of the rich, it is quite liberally used.

That all these three articles are poisonous can be seen from the fact that those who once take to them can never afterwards get on without them. In the old days, I myself used to feel a distinct sense of weariness or langour if I did not get my tea punctually at the usual hour. Once some 400 women and children had gathered together at a certain celebration. The executive committee had resolved against providing tea to the visitors. The women, however, that had assembled there, were in the habit of taking tea at 4 o'clock every evening. The authorities were informed that, if these women were not given their usual tea, they would be too ill to move about, and, needless to say, they had to cancel their original resolution! But some slight delay in the preparation of the tea led to a regular uproar, and the commotion subsided only after the women had had their cup of tea! I can vouch for the authenticity of this incident. In another instance, a certain woman had lost all her digestive powers under the influence of tea, and had become a prey to chronic headaches; but from the moment that she gave up tea her health began steadily to improve. A doctor of the Battersea Municipality in England has declared, after careful investigation, that the brain-tissues of thousands of women in his district have been diseased from excessive use of tea. I have myself come across many instances of health being ruined by tea.

Coffee does some good against *Kapha* (phlegm) and *Vatha* ('wind'), but at the same time it weakens the body by destroying the vital fluid, and by making the blood as thin as water. To those people who advocate coffee on the ground that it is beneficial against "phlegm" and "wind", we would recommend the juice of ginger as even better for the purpose. And, on the other hand, let us remember that the evil effects of coffee are too serious to be counter-balanced by its good. When the blood and the vital fluid are poisoned by a stuff, can there be any hesitation in giving it up altogether?

Cocoa is fully as harmful as coffee, and it contains a poison which deadens the perceptions of the skin.

Those people who recognise the validity of moral considerations in these matters should remember that tea, coffee and cocoa are prepared mostly by labourers under indenture, which is only a fine name for slavery. If we saw with our own eyes the oppressive treatment that is meted out to the labourers in cocoa plantations, we should never again make use of the stuff. Indeed, if we enquire minutely into the methods of preparation of all our articles of food, we shall have to give up 90% of them!

A harmless and healthy substitute for coffee (tea or cocoa) can be prepared as follows. Even habitual coffee-drinkers will be unable to perceive any difference in taste between coffee and this substitute. Good and well-sifted wheat is put into a frying-pan over the fire and well fried, until it has turned completely red, and begun to grow dark in colour. Then it is powdered just like coffee. A spoon of the powder is then put into a cup, and boiling water poured on to it. Preferably keep the thing over the fire for a minute, and add milk and sugar, if necessary, and you get a delicious drink, which is much cheaper and healthier than coffee. Those who want to save themselves the trouble of preparing this powder may get their supply from the *Satyagraha Ashram, Ahmedabad*.

From the point of view of diet, the whole mankind may be divided into *three* broad divisions. (1) The first class, which is the largest, consists of those who, whether by preference or out of necessity, live on an exclusive vegetable diet. Under this division come the best part of India, a large portion of Europe, and China and Japan. The staple diet of the Italians is macaroni, of the Irish potato, of the Scotch oatmeal, and of the Chinese and Japanese rice. (2) The second class consists of those who live on a mixed diet. Under this class come most of the people of England, the richer classes of China and Japan, the richer Mussalmans of India, as well as those rich Hindus who have no religious scruples about taking meat. (3) To the third class belong the uncivilised peoples of the frigid zones, who live on an exclusive meat diet. These are not very numerous, and they also introduce a vegetable element into their diet, wherever they come in contact with the civilised races of Europe. Man, then, can live on three kinds of diet; but it is our duty to consider which of these is the healthiest for us.

An examination of the structure of the human body leads to the conclusion that man is intended by Nature to live on a vegetable diet. There is the closest affinity between the organs of the human body and those of the fruit-eating animals. The monkey, for instance, is so similar to man in shape and structure, and it is a fruit-eating animal. Its teeth and stomach are just like the teeth and stomach of man. From this we may infer that man is intended to live on roots and fruits, and not on meat.

Scientists have found out by experiments that fruits have in them all the elements that are required for man's sustenance. The plantain, the orange, the date, the grape, the apple, the almond, the walnut, the groundnut, the cocoanut,—all these fruits contain a large percentage of nutritious elements. These scientists even hold that there is no need for man to cook his food. They argue that he should be able to subsist very well on food cooked by the Sun's warmth, even as all the lower animals are able to do; and they say that the most nutritious elements in the food are destroyed in the process of cooking, and that those things that cannot be eaten uncooked could not have been intended for our food by Nature.

If this view be correct, it follows that we are at present wasting a lot of our precious time in the cooking of our food. If we could live on uncooked food alone, we should be saving so much time and energy, as well as money, all of which may be utilised for more useful purposes.

Some people will doubtless say that it is idle and foolish to speculate on the possibility of men taking to uncooked food, since there is absolutely no hope of their ever doing it. But we are not considering at present what people will or will not do, but only what they *ought* to do. It is only when we know what the ideal kind of diet is that we shall be able more and more to approximate our actual to the ideal. When we say that a fruit-diet is the best, we do not, of course, expect all men to take to it straightway. We only mean that, *if* they should take to this diet, it would be the best thing for them.

There are many men in England who have tried a pure fruit-diet, and who have recorded the results of their experience. They were people who took to this diet, not out of religious scruples, but simply out of considerations of health. A German doctor has written a bulky volume on the subject, and established the value of a fruit-diet by many arguments and evidences. He has cured many diseases by a fruit-diet combined with open-air life. He goes so far as to say that the people of any country can find all the elements of nutrition in the fruits of their own land.

It may not be out of place to record my own experience in this connection. For the last six months I have been living exclusively on fruits—rejecting even milk and curd. My present dietary consists of plantain, groundnut and olive oil, with some sour fruit like the lime. I cannot say that my experiment has been altogether a success, but a period of six months is all too short to arrive at any definite conclusions on such a vital matter as a complete change of diet. This, however, I can say, that, during this period, I have been able to keep well where others have been attacked by disease, and my physical as well as mental powers are now greater than before. I may not be able to lift heavy loads, but I can now do hard labour for a much longer time without fatigue. I can also do more mental work, and with better persistence and resoluteness. I have tried a fruit-diet on many sickly people, invariably with great advantage. I shall describe these experiences in the section on diseases. Here I will only say that my own experience, as well as my study of the subject, has confirmed me in the conviction that a fruit-diet is the best for us.

As I have already confessed, I do not think for a moment that people will take to a fruit-diet as soon as they read this. It may even be that all that I have written has no effect at all on a single reader, but I believe it to be my bounden duty to set down what I hold to be the right thing to the best of my light.

If however, anybody does wish to try a fruit-diet, he should proceed rather cautiously in order to obtain the best results. He should carefully go through all the chapters of this book, and fully grasp the fundamental principles, before he proceeds to do anything in practice. My request to my readers is that they should reserve their final judgments until they have read through all that I have got to say.

A vegetable diet is the best after a fruit-diet. Under this term we include all kinds of pot-herbs and cereals, as well as milk. Vegetables are not as nutritious as fruits, since they lose part of their efficacy in the process of cooking. We cannot, however, eat uncooked vegetables. We will now proceed to consider which vegetables are the best for us.

Wheat is the best of all the cereals. Man can live on wheat alone, for in it we have in due proportion all the elements of nutrition. Many kinds of edibles can be made of wheat, and they can all be easily digested. The ready-made foods for children that are sold by chemists are also made partly of wheat. Millet and maize belong to the same genus, and cakes and loaves can also be made out of them, but they are inferior to wheat in their food-value. We will now consider the best form in which wheat may be taken. The white "mill flour" that is sold in our bazars is quite useless; it contains no nutriment at all. An English doctor tells us that a dog which was fed solely on this flour died, while other dogs which were fed on better flour remained quite healthy. There is a great demand for loaves made of this flour, since men eat merely to satisfy their palate, and are rarely moved by considerations of health. These loaves are devoid of taste and nutriment, as well as of softness. They become so hard that they cannot be broken by the hand. *The best form of flour is that which is made of well-sifted wheat in the grind-mill at home.* This flour should be used without further sifting. Loaves made of it are quite sweet to the taste, as well as quite soft. It also lasts for a longer time than the "mill flour", since it is far more nutritious, and may be used in smaller quantities.

The loaf sold in the bazars is thoroughly useless. It may be quite white and attractive in appearance, but it is invariably adulterated. The worst of it is that it is made by fermentation. Many persons have testified from experience that fermented dough is harmful to health. Further, these loaves being made by besmearing the oven with fat, they are objectionable to Hindu as well as Mussalman sentiment. To fill the stomach with these bazar loaves instead of preparing good loaves at home is at best a sign of indolence.

Another and an easier way of taking wheat is this. Wheat is ground into coarse grain, which is then well cooked and mixed with milk and sugar. This gives a very delicious and healthy kind of food.

Rice is quite useless as a food. Indeed, it is doubtful if men can subsist upon mere rice, to the exclusion of such nutritious articles as *dhall*, *ghee* and milk. This is not the case with wheat, for man can retain his strength by living on mere wheat boiled in water.

We eat the pot-herbs mainly for their taste. As they have laxative powers, they help to purify the blood up to a limit. Yet they are but varieties of grass, and very hard to digest. Those who partake too much of them have flabby bodies; they suffer very often from indigestion, and go about in search of digestive pills and powders. Hence, if we take them at all, we should do so in moderation.

All the many varieties of pulse are very heavy, and hard of digestion. Their merit is that those who eat them do not suffer from hunger for a long time; but they also lead to indigestion in most cases. Those who do hard labour may be able to digest them, and derive some good out of them. But we who lead a sedentary life should be very chary of eating them.

Dr. Haig, a celebrated writer in England, tells us, on the basis of repeated experiments, that the pulses are injurious to health, since they generate a kind of acid in the system, which leads to several diseases, and a premature old age. His arguments need not be given here, but my own experience goes to confirm his view. Those, however, who are unable or unwilling to eschew the pulses altogether, should use them with great caution.

Almost everywhere in India, the spices and condiments are freely used, as nowhere else in the whole world. Even the African negroes dislike the taste of our *masala*, and refuse to eat food mixed with it. And if the Whites eat *masala*, their stomach gets out of order, and pimples also appear on their faces, as I have found from my own experience. The fact is that *masala* is by no means savoury in itself, but we have so long been accustomed to its use that its flavour appeals to us. But, as has been already explained, it is wrong to eat anything for its mere taste.

How comes it, then, that *masala* is so freely eaten by us? Admittedly, in order to help the digestion, and to be able to eat more. Pepper, mustard, coriander and other condiments have the power of artificially helping the digestion, and generating a sort of artificial hunger. But it would be wrong to to infer from this that all the food has been thoroughly digested, and assimilated into the system. Those who take too much of *masala* are often found to suffer from anaemia, and even from diarrhea. I know a man who even died in the prime of youth out of too much eating of pepper. Hence it is quite necessary to eschew all condiments altogether.

What has been said of *masala* applies also to salt. Most people would be scandalised at this suggestion, but it is a fact established by experience. There is a school in England who even hold the view that salt is more harmful than most condiments. As there is enough of salt in the composition of the vegetables we use, we need not put any extra salt into them. Nature herself has provided just as much salt as is required for the upkeep of our health. All the extra salt that we use is quite superfluous; all of it goes out of the body again in the form of perspiration, or in other ways, and no portion of it seems to have any useful function to perform in the body. One writer even holds that salt poisons the blood. He says that those who use no salt at all have their blood so pure that they are not affected even by snake-bite. We do not know if this is a fact or not, but this much we know from experience, that, in several diseases like piles and asthama, the disuse of salt at once produces appreciably beneficial results. And, on the other hand, I have not come across a single instance of a man being any the worse for not using salt. I myself left off the use of salt two years ago, and I have not only not suffered by it, but have even been benefitted in some respects. I have not now to drink as much water as before, and am more brisk and energetic. The reason for my disuse of salt was a very strange one: for it was occasioned by the illness of somebody else! The person whose illness led to it did not get worse after that, but remained in the same condition; and it is my faith that, if only the diseased person himself had given up the use of salt, he would have recovered completely.

Those who give up salt will also have to give up vegetables and *dhall*. This is a very hard thing to do, as I have found from many tests. I am convinced that vegetables and *dhall* cannot be properly digested without salt. This does not, of course, mean that salt improves the digestion, but it only *appears* to do so, just as pepper does, although ultimately it leads to evil consequences. Of course, the man who entirely gives up the use of salt may feel out of sorts for a few days; but, if he keeps up his spirits, he is bound to be immensely benefitted in the long run.

I make bold to regard even milk as one of the articles to be eschewed! This I do on the strength of my own experience which, however, need not be described here in detail. The popular idea of the value of milk is a pure superstition, but it is so deep-rooted that it is futile to think of removing it. As I have said more than once, I do not cherish the hope that my readers will accept all my views; I do not even believe that all those who accept them in theory will adopt them in practice. Nevertheless, I think it my duty to speak out what I believe to be the truth, leaving my readers to form their own judgments. Many doctors hold the view that milk gives rise to a kind of fever, and many books have been written in support of this view. The disease bearing germs that live in the air rapidly gain an entrance into the milk, and render it poisonous, so that it is very difficult to keep milk in a state of perfect purity. In Africa elaborate rules have been laid down for the conduct of the dairies, saying how the milk should be boiled and preserved, how the vessels should be kept clean, and so on. When so much pains have to be taken in this matter, it is certainly to be considered how far it is worth while to employ milk as an article of food.

Moreover, the purity or otherwise of the milk depends upon the cow's food, and the state of its health. Doctors have testified to the fact that those who drink the milk of consumptive cows fall a prey to consumption themselves. It is very rare to come across a cow that is perfectly healthy. That is to say, perfectly pure milk is very hard to obtain, since it is tainted at its very source. Everybody knows that a child that sucks the breast of its mother contracts any disease that she might be suffering from. And often when a little child is ill, medicine is administered to its mother, so that its effect might reach the child through the milk of her breast. Just in the same way, the health of the man who drinks the milk of a cow will be the same as that of the cow itself. When the use of milk is fraught with so much danger, would it not be the part of wisdom to eschew it altogether, especially when there are excellent substitutes? Olive oil, for instance serves this purpose to some extent; and sweet almond is a most efficient substitute. The almond is first soaked in hot water, and its husk removed. Then it is well crushed, and mixed thoroughly well with water. This gives a drink which contains all the good properties of milk, and is at the same time free from its evil effects.

Now let us consider this question from the point of view of Natural law. The calf drinks its mother's milk only until its teeth have grown; and it begins to eat as soon as it has its teeth. Clearly, this is also what man is intended to do. Nature does not intend us to go on drinking milk after we have ceased to be infants. We should learn to live on fruits like the apple and the almond, or on wheat *roti*, after we have our teeth. Although this is not the place to consider the saving in money that might be effected by giving up milk, it is certainly a point to be kept in mind. Nor is there any need for any of the articles produced from milk. The sourness of lime is quite a good substitute for that of buttermilk; and as for *ghee*, thousands of Indians manage with oil even now.

A careful examination of the structure of the human body shows that meat is not the natural food of man. Dr. Haig and Dr. Kingsford have very clearly demonstrated the evil effects of meat on the body of man. They have shown that meat generates just the same kind of acid in the body as the pulses. It leads to the decay of the teeth, as well as to rheumatism; it also gives rise to evil passions like anger, which, as we have already seen, are but forms of disease.

To sum up, then, we find that those who live on fruits alone are very rare, but it is quite easy to live on a combination of fruits, wheat and olive oil, and it is also eminently conducive to sound health. The plantain comes easy first among the fruits; but the date, the grape, the plum and the orange, to name only a few, are all quite nourishing, and may be taken along with the *roti*. The *roti* does not suffer in taste by being besmeared with olive oil. This diet dispenses with salt, pepper, milk and sugar, and is quite simple and cheap. It is, of course, foolish to eat sugar for its own sake. Too much sweetmeat weakens the teeth, and injures the health. Excellent edibles can be made of wheat and the fruits, and a combination of health and taste secured.

The next question to consider is how much food should be taken, and how many times a day. But, as this is a subject of vital importance, we will devote a separate chapter to it.

CHAPTER VI
HOW MUCH AND HOW MANY TIMES SHOULD WE EAT?

There is a great divergence of opinion among doctors as to the quantity of food that we should take. One doctor holds that we should eat to the utmost of our capacity, and he has calculated the quantities of different kinds of food that we can take. Another holds the view that the food of labourers should differ in quantity as well as in quality from that of persons engaged in mental work, while a third doctor contends that the prince and the peasant should eat exactly the same quantity of food. This much, however, will be generally admitted, that the weak cannot eat just as much as the strong. In the same way, a woman eats less than a man, and children and old men eat less than young men. One writer goes so far as to say that, if only we would masticate our food thoroughly well, so that every particle of it is mixed with the saliva, then we should not have to eat more than five or ten tolas of food. This he says on the basis of numberless experiments, and his book has been sold in thousands. All this shows that it is futile to think of prescribing the quantity of food for men.

Most doctors admit that 99% of human beings eat more than is needed. Indeed, this is a fact of everyday experience, and does not require to be proclaimed by any doctor. There is no fear at all of men ruining their health by eating *too little*; and the great need is for a reduction in the quantity of food that we generally take.

As said above, it is of the utmost importance to masticate the food thoroughly well. By so doing, we shall be able to extract the maximum of nutriment from the minimum of food. Experienced persons point out that the fæces of a man whose food is wholesome, and who does not eat too much, will be small in quantity, quite solid and smooth, dark in colour, and free from all foul smell. The man who does not have such fæces should understand that he has eaten too much of unwholesome food, and has failed to masticate it well. Also, if a man does not get sleep at night, or if his sleep be troubled by dreams, and if his tongue be dirty in the morning, he should know that he has been guilty of excessive eating. And if he has to get up several times at night to make water, it means that he has taken too much liquid food at night. By these and other tests, every man can arrive at the exact quantity of food that is needed for him. Many men suffer from foul breath, which shows that their food has not been well digested. In many cases, again, too much eating gives rise to pimples on the face, and in the nose; and many people suffer from wind in the stomach. The root of all these troubles is, to put it plainly, that we have converted our stomach into a latrine, and we carry this latrine about with us. When we consider the matter in a sober light, we cannot help feeling an unmixed contempt for ourselves. If we want to avoid the sin of over-eating, we should take a vow never to have anything to do with feasts of all kinds. Of course, we should feed those who come to us as guests, but only so as not to violate the laws of health. Do we ever think of inviting our friends to clean their teeth with us, or to take a glass of water? Is not eating as strictly a matter of health as these things? Why, then, should we make so much fuss about it? We have become such gluttons by habit that our tongues are ever craving for abnormal sensations. Hence we think it a sacred duty to cram our guests with rich food, and we cherish the hope that they will do likewise for us, when their turn comes! If, an hour after eating, we ask a clean-bodied friend to smell our mouth, and if he should tell us his exact feelings, we should have to hide our heads in utter shame! But some people are so shameless that they take purgatives soon after eating, that they might be able to eat still more or they even vomit out what they have eaten in order to sit down again to the feast at once!

Since even the best of us are more or less guilty of over-eating, our wise forefathers have prescribed frequent fasts as a religious duty. Indeed, merely from the point of view of health, it will be highly beneficial to fast at least once a fortnight. Many pious Hindus take only one meal a day during the rainy season. This is a practice based upon the soundest hygienic principles. For, when the air is damp and the sky cloudy, the digestive organs are weaker than usual, and hence there should be a reduction in the quantity of food.

And now we will consider how may meals we may take in the day. Numberless people in India are content with only two meals. Those who do hard labour take three meals, but a system of four meals has arisen after the invention of English medicines! Of late, several societies have been formed in England and in America in order to exhort the people to take only two meals a day. They say that we should not take a breakfast early in the morning, since our sleep itself serves the purpose of the breakfast. As soon as we get up in the morning we should prepare to work rather than to eat. We should take our meal only after working for three hours. Those who hold these views take only two meals a day, and do not even take tea in the interval. An experienced doctor by name Deway has written an excellent book on Fasting, in which he has shown the benefits of dispensing with the breakfast. I can also say from my experience that there is absolutely no need to eat more than twice, for a man who has passed the period of youth, and whose body has attained its fullest growth.

CHAPTER VII
EXERCISE

Exercise is as much of a vital necessity for man as air, water and food, in the sense that no man who does not take exercise regularly, can be perfectly healthy. By "exercise" we do not mean merely walking, or games like hockey, football, and cricket; we include under the term all physical and mental activity. Exercise, even as food, is as essential to the mind as to the body. The mind is much weakened by want of exercise as the body, and a feeble mind is, indeed, a form of disease. An athlete, for instance, who is an expert in wrestling, cannot be regarded as a really *healthy* man, unless his mind is equally efficient. As already explained, "a sound mind in a sound body" alone constitutes true health.

Which, then, are those exercises which keep the body and the mind equally efficient? Indeed, Nature has so arranged it that we can be engaged in physical as well as mental work at the same time. The vast majority of men on earth live by field-labour. The farmer has to do strenuous bodily exercise at any cost, for he has to work for 8 or 10 hours, or sometimes even more, in order to earn his bread and clothing. And efficient labour is impossible unless the mind is also in good condition. He has to attend to all the many details of cultivation; he must have a good knowledge of soils and seasons, and perhaps also of the movements of the sun, the moon, and the stars. Even the ablest men will be beaten by the farmer in these matters. He knows the state of his immediate surroundings thoroughly well, he can find the directions by looking at the stars in the night, and tell a great many things from the ways of birds and beasts. He knows, for instance, that rain is about to fall when a particular class of birds gather together, and begin to make noise. He knows as much of the earth and the sky as is necessary for his work. As he has to bring up his children, he must know something of *Dharma Sastra*. Since he lives under the broad open sky, he easily realises the greatness of God.

Of course, all men cannot be farmers, nor is this book written for them. We have however, described the life of the farmer, as we are convinced that it is the *natural life* for man. To the extent to which we deviate from these natural conditions must we suffer in health. From the farmer's life we learn that we should work for at least 8 hours a day, and it should involve mental work as well.

Merchants and others leading a sedentary life have indeed, to do some mental work, but their work is too one-sided and too inadequate to be called *exercise.*

For such people the wise men of the West have devised games like cricket and football, and such minor games as are played at parties and festive gatherings. As for mental work the reading of such books as involve no mental strain is prescribed. No doubt these games do give exercise to the body, but it is a question if they are equally beneficial to the mind. How many of the best players of football and cricket are men of superior mental powers? What have we seen of the mental equipment of those Indian Princes who have earned a distinction as players? On the other hand, how many of the ablest men care to play these games? We can affirm from our experience that there are very few players among those who are gifted with great mental powers. The people of England are extremely fond of games, but their own poet, Kipling, speaks very disparagingly of the mental capacity of the players.

Here in India, however, we have chosen quite a different path! Our men do arduous mental work, but give little or no exercise to the body. Their bodies are enfeebled by excessive mental strain, and they fall a prey to serious diseases; and just when the world expects to benefit by their work, they bid it eternal farewell! Our work should be neither exclusively physical nor exclusively mental, nor such as ministers merely to the pleasure of the moment. The ideal kind of exercise is that which gives vigour to the body as well as to the mind; only such exercise can keep a man truly healthy, and such a man is the farmer.

But what shall he do who is no farmer? The exercise which games like the cricket give is too inadequate, and something else has to be devised. The best thing for ordinary men would be to keep a small garden near the house, and work in it for a few hours every day. Some may ask, "What can we do if the house we live in be not our own?" This is a foolish question to ask, for, whoever may be the owner of the house, he cannot object to his ground being improved by digging and cultivation. And we shall have the satisfaction of feeling that we have helped to keep somebody else's ground neat and clean. Those who do not find time for such exercise or who may not like it, may resort to walking, which is the next best exercise. Truly has this been described as the Queen of all exercises. The main reason why our *Sadhus* and *Fakirs* are strong as a class is that they go about from one end of the country to the other only on foot. Thoreau, the great American writer, has said many remarkable things on walking as an exercise. He says that the writings of those who keep indoors and never go out into the open air, will be as weak as their bodies. Referring to his own experience, he says that all his best works were written when he was walking the most. He was such an inveterate walker that four or five hours a day was quite an ordinary thing with him! Our passion for exercise should become so strong that we cannot bring ourselves to dispense with it on any account. We hardly realise how weak and futile is our mental work when unaccompanied by hard physical exercise. Walking gives movement to every portion of the body, and ensures vigorous circulation of the blood; for, when we walk fast, fresh air is inhaled into the lungs. Then there is the inestimable joy that natural objects give us, the joy that comes from a contemplation of the beauties of nature. It is, of course, useless to walk along lanes and streets, or to take the same path every day. We should go out into the fields and forests where we can have a taste of Nature. Walking a mile or two is no walking at all; at least ten or twelve miles are necessary for exercise. Those who cannot walk so much every day can at least do so on Sundays. Once a man who was suffering from indigestion went to the doctor to take medicine. He was advised to walk a little every day, but he pleaded that he was too weak to walk at all. Then the doctor took him into his carriage for a drive. On the way he deliberately dropped his whip, and the sick man, out of courtesy, got down to take it. The doctor, however, drove on without waiting for him, and the poor man had to trudge behind the carriage. When the doctor was satisfied that he had walked long enough, he took him into the carriage again, and explained that it was a device adopted to make him walk. As the man had begun to feel hungry by this time, he realised the value of the doctor's advice, and forgot the affair of the whip. He then went home and had a hearty meal. Let those who are suffering from indigestion and kindred diseases try for themselves, and they will at once realise the value of walking as an exercise.

CHAPTER VIII
DRESS

Dress is also a matter of health to a certain extent. European ladies, for instance, have such queer notions of beauty that their dress is contrived with a view to straitening the waist and the feet, which, in its turn, leads to several diseases. The feet of Chinese women are deliberately straitened to such an extent that they are smaller even than the feet of our little children, and, as a result, their health is injured. These two instances show how the health may be affected by the nature of the dress. But the choice of our dress does not rest always in our hands, for we have perforce to adopt the manners of our elders. The chief object of dress has been forgotten, and it has come to be regarded as indicative of a man's religion, country, race and profession. In this state of things, it is very difficult to discuss the question of dress strictly from the point of view of health, but such a discussion must necessarily do us good. Under the term dress, we include all such things as boots and shoes, as well as jewellery and the like.

What is the chief object of dress? Man in his primitive state had no dress at all; he went about naked, and exposing almost the whole body. His skin was firm and strong, he was able to stand sun and shower, and never once suffered from cold and kindred ailments. As has already been explained, we inhale the air not only through the nostrils, but also through the numberless pores of the skin. So when we cover the body with clothing, we are preventing this natural function of the skin. But when the people of the colder countries grew more and more indolent, they began to feel the need to cover their bodies. They were no longer able to stand the cold, and the use of dress came into being, until at length it came to be looked upon not merely as a necessity, but as an ornament. Subsequently it has also come to be regarded as an indication of country, race etc.

In fact, Nature herself has provided an excellent covering for us in our skin. The idea that the body looks unseemly in undress is absurd, for the very best pictures are those that display the naked body. When we cover up the most ordinary parts of our body, it is as though we felt ashamed of them in their natural condition, and as though we found fault with Nature's own arrangement. We think it a duty to go on multiplying the trappings and ornaments for our body, as we grow richer and richer. We 'adorn' our body in all sorts of hideous ways, and pride ourselves on our handsomeness! If our eyes were not blinded by foolish habit, we should see that the body looks most handsome only in its nakedness, as it enjoys its best health only in that condition. Dress, indeed, detracts from the natural beauty of the body. But, not content with dress alone, man began to wear jewels also. This is mere madness, for it is hard to understand how these jewels can add an iota to the body's natural beauty. But women have gone beyond all bounds of sense or decency in this matter. They are not ashamed to wear anklets which are so heavy that they can hardly lift their feet, or to pierce their nose and ears hideously for putting on rings, or to stud their wrists and fingers with rings and bracelets of several kinds. These ornaments only serve to help the accumulation of dirt in the body; there is indeed no limit to the dirt on the nose and ears. We mistake this filthiness for beauty, and throw money away to secure it; and we do not even shrink from putting our lives at the mercy of thieves. There is no limit to the pains we take to satisfy the silly notions of vanity that we have so sedulously cultivated. Women, indeed, have become so infatuated that they are not prepared to remove the ear-ring even if the ears are diseased; even if the hand is swollen and suffering from frightful pain, they would not remove the bracelets; and they are unwilling to remove the ring from a swollen finger, since they imagine that their beauty would suffer by so doing!

A thorough reform in dress is by no means an easy matter, but it is surely possible for all of us to renounce our jewels and all superfluous clothing. We may keep some few things for the sake of convention, and throw off all the rest. Those who are free from the superstition that dress is an ornament can surely effect many changes in their dress, and keep themselves in good health.

Now-a-days the notion has gained ground that European dress is necessary for maintaining our decency and prestige! This is not the place to discuss this question in detail. Here it will be enough to point out that, although the dress of Europeans might be good enough for the cold countries of Europe, it is hopelessly unsuited to India. Indian dress, alone, can be good for Indians, whether they be Hindu or Musalman. Our dress being loose and open, air is not shut out; and being white for the most part, it does not absorb the heat. Black dress feels hot, since all the sun's rays are absorbed into it, and, in its turn, into the body.

The practice of covering the head with the turban has become quite common with us. Nevertheless we should try to keep the head bare as far as possible. To grow the hair, and to dress it by combing and brushing, parting in the middle and so on, is nothing short of barbarous. Dust and dirt, as well as nits and lice, accumulate in the hair, and if a boil were to arise on the head, it cannot be properly treated. Especially for those who use a turban, it would be stupid to grow the hair.

The feet also are common agents of disease. The feet of those who wear boots and shoes grow dirty, and begin to exude a lot of stinking perspiration. So great is the stink that those who are sensitive to smells will hardly be able to stand by the side of one who is removing his shoes and socks. Our common names for the shoe speak of it as the "protector of the feet" and the "enemy of the thorn" showing that shoes should be worn only when we have to walk along a thorny path, or over very cold or hot ground, and that only the soles should be covered, and not the entire feet. And this purpose is served excellently well by the *sandal*. Some people who are accustomed to the use of shoes often suffer from headaches, of pain in the feet, or weakness of the body. Let them try the experiment of walking with bare feet, and then they will at once find out the benefit of keeping the feet bare, and free from sweat by exposure to the air.

CHAPTER IX
SEXUAL RELATIONS

I would specially request those who have carefully read through the book so far to read through this chapter with even greater care, and ponder well over its subject-matter. There are still several more chapters to be written, and they will, of course, be found useful in their own way. But not one of them is nearly as important as this. As I have already said, there is not a single matter mentioned in this book which is not based on my personal experience, or which I do not believe to be strictly true.

Many are the keys to health, and they are all quite essential; but the one thing needful, above all others, is *Brahmacharya*. Of course, pure air, pure water, and wholesome food do contribute to health. But how can we be healthy if we expend all the health that we acquire? How can we help being paupers if we spend all the money that we earn? There can be no doubt that men and women can never be virile or strong unless they observe true *Brahmacharya*.

What do we mean by *Brahmacharya*? We mean by it that men and women should refrain from enjoying each other. That is to say, they should not touch each other with a carnal thought, they should not think of it even in their dreams. Their mutual glances should be free from all suggestion of carnality. The hidden strength that God has given us should be conserved by rigid self-discipline, and transmitted into energy and power,—not merely of body, but also of mind and soul.

But what is the spectacle that we actually see around us? Men and women, old and young, without exception, are seen entangled in the coils of sensuality. Blinded by lust, they lose all sense of right and wrong. I have myself seen even boys and girls behaving like mad men under its fatal influence. I too have behaved likewise under similar influences, and it could not well be otherwise. For the sake of a momentary pleasure, we sacrifice in an instant all the stock of vitality that we have accumulated. The infatuation over, we find ourselves in a miserable condition. The next morning, we feel hopelessly weak and tired, and the mind refuses to do its work. Then, we try to remedy the mischief by taking all sorts of 'nervine tonics' and put ourselves under the doctor's mercy for repairing the waste, and for recovering the capacity for enjoyment. So the days pass and the years, until at length old age comes upon us, and finds us utterly emasculated in body and in mind.

But the law of Nature is just the reverse of this. The older we grow, the keener should grow our intellect also; the longer we live, the greater should be our capacity to transmit the fruits of our accumulated experience to our fellowmen. And such is indeed the case with those who have been true *Brahmacharies*. They know no fear of death, and they do not forget good even in the hour of death; nor do they indulge in vain complaints. They die with a smile on their lips, and boldly face the day of judgment. They are the true men and women; and of them alone can it be said that they have conserved their health.

We hardly realise the fact that incontinence is the root-cause of all the vanity, anger, fear and jealousy in the world. If our mind is not under our control, if we behave once or more every day more foolishly than even little children, what sins may we not commit consciously or unconsciously? How can we pause to think of the consequences of our actions, however vile or sinful they may be?

But you may ask, "Who has ever seen a true *Brahmachary* in this sense? If all men should turn *Brahmacharies*, would not humanity be extinct, and the whole world go to rack and ruin?" We will leave aside the religious aspect of this question, and discuss it simply from the secular point of view. To my mind, these questions only bespeak our weakness and our cowardliness. We have not the strength of will to observe *Brahmacharya*, and, therefore, set about finding pretexts for evading our duty. The race of true *Brahmacharies* is by no means extinct; but, if they were to be had merely for the asking, of what value would *Brahmacharya* be? Thousands of hardy labourers have to go and dig deep into the bowels of the earth in search of diamonds, and at length they get perhaps merely a handful of them out of heaps and heaps of rock. How much greater, then, should be the labour involved in the discovery of the infinitely more precious diamond of a *Brahmachary*? If the observance of *Brahmacharya* should mean the ruin of the world, why should we regret it? Are we God that we should be so anxious about its future? He who created it will surely see to its preservation. It is none of our business to enquire if other people practise *Brahmacharya* or not. When we turn merchant or lawyer or doctor, do we ever pause to consider what the fate of the world would be if all men were to do likewise? The true *Brahmachary* will, in the long run, discover for himself answers to such questions.

But how can men engrossed by the cares of the material world put these ideas into practice? What shall the married people do? What shall they do who have children? And what shall be done by those people who cannot control their lust? The best solution for all such difficulties has already been given. We should keep this ideal constantly before us, and try to approximate to it more and more to the utmost of our capacity. When little children are taught to write the letters of the alphabet, we show them the perfect shapes of the letters, and they try to reproduce them as best they can. Just in the same way, if we steadily work up to the ideal of *Brahmacharya*, we may ultimately succeed in realising it. What if we have married already? The law of Nature is that *Brahmacharya* may be broken only when the husband and wife feel a strong desire for a child. Those who, remembering this law, violate *Brahmacharya* once in four or five years cannot be said to be slaves to lust, nor can they appreciably lose their stock of vitality. But, alas, how rare are those men and women who yield to the sexual craving merely for the sake of an offspring! The vast majority, who may be numbered in thousands, turn to sexual enjoyment merely to satisfy their carnal passion, with the result that children are born to them quite against their will. In the madness of sexual passion, we give no thought to the consequences of our acts. In this respect, men are even more to blame than women. The man is blinded so much by his lust that he never cares to remember that his wife is weak and incapable of rearing a child. In the West indeed, people have trespassed even against the claims of common decency. They indulge in sexual pleasures, and devise measures in order to evade the responsibilities of parenthood. Many books have been written on this subject, and a regular trade is being carried on in providing the means of preventing conception. We are as yet free from this sin, but we do not shrink from imposing the heavy burden of maternity on our women, and we are not concerned even to find that our children are weak, impotent and imbecile. Every time we get children, we bless Providence, and so seek to hide from ourselves the wickedness of our acts. Should we not rather deem it a sign of God's anger to have children who are weak, sensual, crippled and impotent? Is it a matter for joy that mere boys and girls should have children? Is it not rather a curse of God? We all know that the premature fruit of a too young plant weakens the parent, and so we try all means of delaying the appearance of fruit. But we sing hymns of praise and thanks-giving to God when a child is born of a boy-father and a girl-mother! Could anything be more dreadful? Do we think that the world is going to be saved by the countless swarms of such impotent children endlessly multiplying in India or elsewhere in the world? Verily we are, in this respect, far worse than even the lower animals; for, the bull and the cow are brought together solely with the object of having a calf. Man and woman should regard it as sacred duty to keep apart from the moment of conception up to the time when the child has ceased to suck its mother's breast. But we go on in our merry fashion blissfully forgetful of this sacred obligation. This incurable disease enfeebles our mind and leads us to an early grave, after making us drag a miserable existence for a short while. Married people should understand the true function of marriage, and should not violate the law of *Brahmacharya* except with a view to having a child for the continuation of the race.

But this is so difficult under our present conditions of life. Our diet, our ways of life, our common talk, and our environments are all equally calculated to rouse and keep alive our sensual appetite; and sensuality is like a poison, eating into our vitals. Some people may doubt the possibility of our being able to free ourselves from this bondage. This book is written not for those who go about with such doubtings of heart, but only for those who are really in earnest, and who have the courage to take active steps for their improvement. Those who are quite content with their present abject condition may even be offended to read all this; but I hope this will be of some service to those who are heartily disgusted with their own miserable existence.

From all that has been said, it follows that those who are still unmarried should try to remain so; but, if they cannot help marrying, they should do so as late as possible. Young men, for instance, should take a vow to remain unmarried till the age of 25 or 30. We shall not explain here all the benefits other than physical that result from this; but those who want to enjoy them can do so for themselves.

My request to those parents who may read these pages is that they should not tie a mill-stone round the necks of their sons by marrying them in their teens. They should look also to the welfare of their sons, and not only to their own interests. They should throw aside all silly notions of caste-pride or 'respectability', and cease to indulge in such heartless practices. Let them, rather, if they are true well-wishers of their children, look to their physical, mental and moral improvements. What greater disservice can they do to their sons than compelling them to enter upon a married life, with all its tremendous responsibilities and cares, even while they are mere boys?

Then again, the true laws of health demand that the man that loses his wife, as well as the woman that loses her husband, should remain single ever after. There is a difference of opinion among doctors as to whether young men and women need ever let their vital fluid escape, some answering the question in the affirmative, others in the negative. But this cannot justify our taking advantage of it for sensual enjoyment. I can affirm, without the slightest hesitation, from my own experience as well as that of others, that sexual enjoyment is not only not necessary for the preservation of health, but is positively detrimental to it. All the strength of body and mind that has taken long to acquire, is lost altogether by the escape of the vital fluid, and it takes a long time to regain this lost strength, and even then there is no saying that it can be thoroughly recovered. A broken vessel may be made to do its work after mending, but it can never be anything but a broken vessel.

As has already been pointed out, the preservation of our vitality is impossible without pure air, pure water, pure and wholesome food, as well as pure thoughts. So vital indeed is the relation between our health and the life that we lead that we can never be perfectly healthy unless we lead a clean life. The earnest man who, forgetting the errors of the past, begins to live a life of purity will be able to reap the fruit of it straightway. Those who have practised true *Brahmacharya* even for a short period will have seen how their body and mind improve steadily in strength and power, and they will not, at any cost, be willing to part with this treasure. I have myself been guilty of lapses even after having fully understood the value of *Brahmacharya*, and have, of course, paid dearly for it. I am filled with shame and remorse when I think of the terrible contrast between my condition before and after these lapses. But from the errors of the past I have now learnt to preserve this treasure in tact, and I fully hope, with God's grace, to continue to preserve it in the future; for I have in my own person, witnessed the inestimable benefits of *Brahmacharya*. I was married early in life, and had become the father of children as a mere youth. When, at length, I awoke to the reality of my situation, I found myself sunk in the lowest depths of degradation. I shall consider myself amply rewarded for writing these pages if at least a single reader is able to take warning from my failings and experiences, and to profit thereby. Many people have told me (and I also believe it) that I am full of energy and enthusiasm, and that my mind is by so means weak; some even accuse me of rashness. There is disease in my body as well as in my mind; nevertheless, when compared with my friends, I may call myself perfectly healthy and strong. If even after twenty years of sensual enjoyment, I have been able to reach this state, how much better should I have been if only I had kept myself pure during those twenty years as well? It is my full conviction that, if only I had lived a life of *Brahmacharya* all through, my energy and enthusiasm would have been a thousandfold greater and I should have been able to devote them all to the furtherance of my country's cause as of my own. If this can be affirmed of an ordinary man like myself, how much more wonderful must be the gain in power,—physical, mental, as well as moral—that unbroken *Brahmacharya* can bring to us!

When so strict is the law of *Brahmacharya*, what shall we say of those guilty of the unpardonable sin of illegitimate sexual enjoyment? The evil that arises from adultery and prostitution is a vital question of religion and morality and cannot be fully dealt with in a treatise on health. Here we are only concerned to point out how thousands who are guilty of these sins are afflicted by syphilis and other unmentionable diseases. The inflexible decree of Providence happily condemns these wretches to a life of unmitigated suffering. Their short span of life is spent in abject bondage to quacks in a futile quest after a remedy that will rid them of their suffering. If there were no adultery at all, there would be no work for at least 50% of doctors. So inextricably indeed has venereal disease caught mankind in its clutches that even the best doctors have been forced to admit that, so long as adultery and prostitution continue, there is no hope for the human race. The medicines for these diseases are so poisonous that, although they may appear to have done some good for the time being, they give rise to other and still more terrible diseases which are handed down from generation to generation.

In concluding this chapter, we will briefly point out how married people can preserve their *Brahmacharya* intact. It is not enough to observe the laws of health as regards air, water and food. The man should altogether cease to sleep in privacy with his wife. Little reflection is needed to show that the only possible motive for privacy between man and wife is the desire for sexual enjoyment. They should sleep apart at night, and be incessantly engaged in good works during the day. They should read such books as fill them with noble thoughts and meditate over the lives of great men, and live in the constant realisation of the fact that sensual enjoyment is the root of all disease. Whenever they feel a prompting for enjoyment, they should bathe in cold water, so that the heat of passion may be cooled down, and be refined into the energy of virtuous activity. This is a hard thing to do, but we have been born into this world that we might wrestle with difficulties and temptations, and conquer them; and he who has not the will to do it can never enjoy the supreme blessing of true health.

PART II
SOME SIMPLE TREATMENTS

CHAPTER I
AIR-TREATMENT

We have now done with the discussion of the foundations of health, as well as the means of its preservation. If all men and women were to obey all the laws of health, and practice strict Brahmacharya, there would be no need at all for the chapters which follow, for such men and women would then be free from all ailments, whether of the body or of the mind. But where can such men and women be found? Where are they who have not been afflicted by disease? The more strictly, however, we observe the laws which have been explained in this book, the more shall we be free from disease. But when diseases do attack us, it is our duty to deal with them properly, and the following chapters are intended to show how to do it.

Pure air, which is so essential to the preservation of health, is also essential to the cure of diseases. If, for instance, a man who is suffering from gout is treated with air heated by steam, he perspires profusely, and his joints are eased. This kind of vapour-treatment is known as "Turkish Bath."

If a man who is suffering from high fever is stripped naked, and made to sleep in the open air, there is an immediate fall in the temperature, and he feels a distinct relief. And if, when he feels cold, he is wrapped in a blanket, he perspires at once, and the fever ceases. But what we generally do is just the reverse of this. Even if the patient is willing to remain in the open air, we close all the doors and windows of the room in which he lies, and cover his whole body (including the head and ears) with blankets, with the result that he is frightened, and is rendered still weaker. If the fever is the outcome of too much heat, the sort of air-treatment described above is perfectly harmless, and its effect can be instantly felt. Of course, care should be taken that the patient does not begin to shiver in the open air. If he cannot remain naked, he may well be covered with blankets.

Change of air is an effective remedy for latent fever and other diseases. The common practice of taking a change of air is only an application of the principle of air-treatment. We often change our residence in the belief that a house constantly infested by disease is the resort of evil spirits. This is a mere delusion, for the real "evil spirits" in such cases are the foul air inside the house. A change of residence ensures a change of air, and with it the cure of the diseases brought on by it. Indeed, so vital is the relation between health and air that the good or evil effects of even a slight change are instantaneously felt. For a change of air the rich can afford to go to distant places, but even the poor can go from one village to another, or at least from one house to another. Even a change of room in the same house often brings great relief to a sick man. But, of course, care should be taken to see that the change of air is really for the better. Thus, for instance, a disease that has been brought on by damp air cannot be cured by a change to a damper locality. It is because sufficient attention is not paid to simple precautions like this that a change of air is often so ineffectual.

This chapter has been devoted to some simple instances of the application of air to the treatment of disease, while the chapter on Air in Part I of this book contains a general consideration of the value of pure air to health. Hence I would request my readers to read these two chapters side by side.

CHAPTER II
WATER-CURE

Since air is invisible, we cannot perceive the wonderful way in which it does its work. But the work of water and its curative effects can be easily seen and understood.

All people know something of the use of steam as a curative agent. We often employ it in cases of fever, and very often severe headaches can be cured only by its application. In cases of rheumatic pain in the joints, rapid relief is obtained by the use of steam followed by a cold bath. Boils and ulcers not cured by simple dressing with ointments can be completely healed by the application of steam.

In case of extreme fatigue, a steam-bath or a hot-water bath immediately followed by a cold bath will be found very effective. So too, in cases of sleeplessness, instant relief is often obtained by sleeping in the open air after a steam-bath followed by a cold bath.

Hot water can always be used as a substitute for steam. When there is severe pain in the stomach, instant relief is obtained by warming with a bottle filled with boiling water placed over a thick cloth wrapped round the waist. Whenever there is a desire to vomit, it can be done by drinking plenty of hot water. Those who are suffering from constipation often derive great benefit by drinking a glass of hot water either at bedtime or soon after rising and cleaning the teeth in the morning. Sir Gordon Spring attributed his excellent health to the practice of drinking a glass of hot water every day before going to bed and after getting up in the morning. The bowels of many people move only after taking tea in the morning, and they foolishly suppose that it is the tea which has produced this effect. But, as a matter of fact, tea only does harm, and it is really the hot water in the tea that moves the bowels.

A special kind of cot is often used for steam-baths, but it is not quite essential. A spirit or kerosine oil stove, or a wood or coal fire, should be kept burning under an ordinary cane chair. Over the fire should be placed a vessel of water with the mouth covered; and over the chair a sheet or blanket is so spread that it may hang down in the front and protect the patient from the heat of the fire. Then the patient should be seated in the chair and wrapped round with sheets or blankets. Then the vessel should be uncovered, so that the patient may be exposed to the steam issuing from it. Our common practice of covering the head also of the patient is a needless precaution. The heat of the steam presses through the body right up to the head, and gives rise to profuse perspiration on the face. If the patient is too weak to sit up, he may be made to lie down on a cot with interstices, taking care to see that none of the steam escapes. Of course, care should also be taken to see that the patient's clothes or the blankets used do not catch fire; and due consideration should be paid to the state of the patient's health, as an inconsiderate application of steam is fraught with danger. The patient, indeed, feels weak after a steam bath, but this weakness does not last long. Too frequent use of steam, however, enfeebles the constitution, and it is of the highest importance to apply steam with due deliberation. Steam may also be applied to any single part of the body; in cases of headache, for instance, there is no need to expose the whole body to the steam. The head should be held just over a narrow-mouthed jar of boiling water, and wrapped round with a cloth. Then the steam should be inhaled through the nose so that it may ascend into the head. If the nasal passage is blocked, it will also be opened by this process. Likewise, if there be inflamation in any part of the body, it alone need be exposed to the steam.

Very few realise the curative value of cold water, in spite of the fact that it is even more valuable in this respect than hot water, and can be made use of by even the weakest persons. In fever, small-pox, and skin-diseases, the application of a sheet dipped in cold water is very beneficial, and often produces startling results; and anybody may try it without the least risk. Dizziness or delirium can be instantly relieved by tying round the head a cloth dipped in melted ice. People suffering from constipation often derive great benefit by tying round the stomach for some time a piece of cloth dipped in melted ice. Involuntary seminal discharges can also be often prevented by the same means. Bleeding in any part of the body may be stopped by the application of a bandage dipped in ice-cold water. Bleeding from the nose is stopped by pouring cold water over the head. Nasal diseases, cold and headache, may be cured by drawing pure cold water up the nose. The water may be drawn through one nostril and discharged through the other, or drawn through both nostrils and discharged through the mouth. There is no harm in the water going even into the stomach provided the nostrils are clean. And indeed, this is the best way to keep the nostrils clean. Those who are unable to draw the water up the nostrils may use a syringe, but after a few attempts, it can be done quite easily. All should learn to do this, since it is very simple, and at the same time a most effective remedy against headaches, bad smells in the nose, as well as dirty accumulations in the nasal passage.

Many people are afraid of taking an enema, and some even think that the body is weakened by it; but such fears are baseless. There is no more effective means of producing an instant evacuation of the bowels. It has proved effective in many diseases where all other remedies have been futile; it thoroughly cleans the bowels, and prevents the accumulation of poisonous matter. If those who suffer from rheumatic complaints or indigestion or pains caused by an unhealthy condition of the bowels take an enema of 2 lbs. of water, they would see how instantaneous is its effect. One writer on this subject says that once he was suffering from chronic indigestion and, all remedies proving futile; he had grown emaciated, but the application of the enema at once restored him his appetite, and altogether cured him of his complaint in a few days. Even ailments like jaundice can be cured by the application of the enema. If the enema has to be frequently employed, cold water should be used, for the repeated use of hot water is likely to enfeeble the constitution.

Dr. Louis Kuhne of Germany has, after repeated experiments, arrived at the conclusion that water-cure is the best for all diseases. His books on this subject are so popular that they are now available in almost all the languages of the world, including those of India. He contends that the abdomen is the seat of all diseases. When there is too much heat in the abdomen, it manifests itself in the form of fever, rheumatism, eruptions on the body, and the like. The efficacy of water-cure had, indeed, been recognised by several people long before Kuhne, but it was he who, for the first time, pointed out the common origin of all diseases. His views need not be accepted by us in their entirety, but it is an undoubted fact that his principles and methods have proved effective in many diseases. To give only one instance out of many that have come within my experience, in a bad case of rheumatism, a thorough cure was effected by Kuhne's system, after all other remedies had been tried, and had proved utterly ineffectual.

Dr. Kuhne holds that the heat in the abdomen abates by the application of cold water, and has, therefore, prescribed the bathing of the abdomen and the surrounding parts with thoroughly cold water. And for the greater convenience of bathing, he has devised a special kind of tin bath. This, however, is not quite indispensable; the tin tubs of an oval shape and of different sizes to suit people of different heights, available in our bazaars, will do equally well. The tub should be filled three-fourths with cold water, and the patient should seat himself in it in such a fashion that his feet and the upper part of the body remain outside the water, and the rest of the body up to the hips inside it. The feet may preferably be placed on a low foot-stool. The patient should sit in the water quite naked, but, if he feels cold, the feet and the upper part of the body should be covered with a blanket. If a shirt is worn, it should be kept entirely outside the water. The bath should be taken in a room where there is plenty of fresh air and light. The patient should then slowly rub (or cause to be rubbed) the abdomen with a small rough towel from 5 to 30 minutes or more. The effect is instantly felt in most cases. In cases of rheumatism, the wind in the stomach escapes in the form of eructations and the like, and in cases of fever, the thermometre falls by one or two degrees. The bowels are readily cleaned by this process; fatigue disappears; sleeplessness is removed, and extreme drowsiness gives place to vigour. This contrariness of result is more apparent than real; for want of sleep, and the excess of it, are both brought on by the same cause. So too, dysentery and constipation, which are both the outcome of indigestion, are cured by this method. Piles of long standing can also be got rid of by this bath, with proper regulation of diet. Those who are troubled by the necessity for constant spitting should at once resort to this treatment for a cure. By its means the weak can become strong; and even chronic rheumatism has been cured by it. It is also an effective remedy for haemorrhages, headaches, and blood-poisoning. Kuhne prescribes it as an invaluable remedy even for diseases like the cancer. A pregnant woman who takes to it regularly will have an easy child-birth. In short, all persons, without distinction of age or sex, can take to it with advantage.

There is another kind of bath, known as the "Wet-Sheet-Pack", which is an unfailing remedy for various diseases. This bath is taken in the following manner. A table or chair is placed in the open air, big enough to allow of the patient lying on it at full length. On it are spread (hanging on either side) some four blankets, less or more according to the state of the weather. Over them are spread two white thick sheets well dipped in cold water, and a pillow is placed under the blankets at one end. Then the patient is stripped naked (with the exception of a small waist-cloth, if he so wishes), and made to lie down on the sheets, with his hands placed in the arm-pits. Then the sheets and blankets are, one after another, wrapped round his body, taking care that the parts hanging under the feet are well tucked in so as to cover them. If the patient is exposed to the sun, a wet cloth is put over his head and face, keeping the nose always open. At first the patient will experience some shivering, but this will soon give place to an agreeably warm sensation. He can lie in this position from 5 minutes to an hour or more. After a time he begins to perspire, or at times falls asleep. Soon after coming out of the sheets he should bathe in cold-water. This is an excellent remedy for small-pox and fever, and skin-diseases like the itch, the ringworm, and pimples and blotches. Even the worst forms of chicken-pox and small-pox are completely cured by this process. People can easily learn to take the "Wet-Sheet-Pack" themselves, and to apply it to others, and can thus see for themselves its wonderful effect. As the whole dirt of the body sticks to the sheets in the process of taking this bath, they ought not to be used again without being well washed in boiling water.

Needless to say, the full benefit of these baths cannot be derived unless the rules already mentioned as to diet, exercise and the like are strictly observed. If a rheumatic patient, for instance, were to take to Kuhne's bath or to the "Wet-Sheet-Pack," while eating unwholesome food, living in impure air, and neglecting his exercise, how can he possibly derive any good out of it? It is only when accompanied by strict observance of all the laws of health that water-cure can be of any effect; and when so employed, its effects are sure and immediate.

CHAPTER III
THE USE OF EARTH

We will now proceed to describe the curative properties of earth, which are, in some cases, even more remarkable than those of water. That earth should have such properties need not cause us any surprise, for our own body is compounded of the earthly element. Indeed, we do make use of earth as a purifying agent. We wash the ground with earth to remove bad smells, we put it over decaying matter to prevent the pollution of the air, we wash our hands with it, and even employ it to clean the private parts. Yogis besmear their bodies with it; some people use it as a cure for boils and ulcers; and dead bodies are buried in the earth so that they may not vitiate the atmosphere. All this shows that earth has many valuable properties as a purifying and curative agent.

Just as Dr. Kuhne has devoted special attention to the subject of water-cure, another German doctor has made a special study of earth and its properties. He goes so far as to say that it can be used with success in the treatment of even the most complicated diseases. He says that once in a case of snake-bite, where everybody else had given up the man for dead, he restored him to life by causing him to be covered up with earth for some time. There is no reason to doubt the veracity of this report. It is well known that great heat is generated in the body by burying it in the earth; and although we cannot explain how exactly the effect is produced, it is undeniable that earth does possess the property of absorbing the poison. Indeed, every case of snake-bite may not be cured in this way; but it should certainly be tried in every case. And I can say from my own experience that, in cases of scorpion-sting and the like, the use of mud is particularly beneficial.

I have myself tried with success the following forms of earth-cure. Constipation, dysentery, and chronic stomach-ache have been cured by the use of a mud-poultice over the abdomen for two or three days. Instant relief has been obtained in cases of headache by applying a mud-bandage round the head. Sore eye has also been cured by the same method; hurts of all kinds, whether accompanied by inflammation or not, have been healed likewise. In the old days I could not keep well without a regular use of Eno's Fruit-salt and the like. But, since 1904, when I learnt the value of earth-cure, I have had not a single occasion to use them. A mud-poultice over the abdomen and the head, gives distinct relief in a state of high fever. Skin-diseases like the itch, the ringworm, and boils, have been cured with the use of mud, though no doubt ulcers from which pus issues are not so easily cured. Burns and scalds are likewise healed by mud, which also prevents inflammation. Piles, too, are cured by the same treatment. When the hands and feet become red and swollen owing to frost, mud is an unfailing remedy, and pain in the joints is also relieved by it. From these and other experiments in mud-cure, I have come to the conclusion that earth is an invaluable element in the domestic treatment of diseases.

All kinds of earth are not, of course, equally beneficial. Dry earth dug out from a clean spot has been found the most effective. It should not be too sticky. Mud which is midway between sand and clay is the best. It should, of course, be free from cow-dung and other rubbish. It should be well sifted in a fine sieve, and then soaked in cold water to the consistency of well-kneaded dough before use. Then it should be tied up in a piece of clean, unstarched cloth, and used in the form of a thick poultice. The poultice should be removed before the mud begins to dry up; ordinarily it will last from two to three hours. Mud once used should never be used again, but a cloth once used can be used again, after being well washed, provided it is free from blood and other dirty matter. If the poultice has to be applied to the abdomen, it should first be covered over with a warm cloth. Everybody should keep a tinful of earth ready for use, so as not to have to hunt for it whenever an occasion arises for its use. Otherwise, much precious time may be wasted in cases (as of scorpion-sting) where delay would be dangerous.

CHAPTER IV
FEVER AND ITS CURE

We now pass on to consider some particular diseases and the means of curing them. And first, fever.

We generally apply the term "fever" to a condition of heat in the body, but English doctors have distinguished many varieties of this disease, each with its own system of treatment. But, following the common practice and the principles elaborated in these chapters, we may say that all fevers can be cured in one and the same manner. I have tried this single treatment for all varieties from simple fever up to Bubonic Plague, with invariably satisfactory results. In 1904, there was a severe outbreak of plague among the Indians in South Africa. It was so severe that, out of 23 persons that were affected, as many as 21 died within the space of 24 hours; and of the remaining two, who were removed to the hospital, only one survived, and that one was the man to whom was applied the mud-poultice. We cannot, of course, conclude from this that it was the mud-poultice that saved him, but, in any case, it is undeniable that it did him no harm. They were both suffering from high fever brought on by inflammation of the lungs, and had been rendered unconscious. The man on whom was tried the mud-poultice was so bad that he was spitting blood, and I afterwards learnt from the doctor that he had been insufficiently fed on milk alone.

As most fevers are caused by disorders of the bowels, the very first thing to do is to starve the patient. It is a mere superstition that a weak man will get weaker by starving. As we have already seen, only that portion of our food is really useful which is assimilated into the blood, and the remainder only clogs the bowels. In fever the digestive organs are very weak, the tongue gets coated, and the lips are hard and dry. If any food is given to the patient in this condition, it will remain undigested and aid the fever. Starving the patient gives his digestive organs time to perform their work; hence the need to starve him for a day or two. At the same time, he should take at least two baths every day according to the Kuhne's system. If he is too weak or ill to bathe, a mud-poultice should be applied to his abdomen. If the head aches or feels too hot, a poultice should also be applied to the head. The patient should, as far as possible, be placed in the open air, and should be well covered. At meal-time, he should be given the juice of lime, well filtered and mixed with cold or boiling water, and if possible, without any sugar. This has a very beneficial effect, and should alone be given if the patient's teeth can bear its sourness. Afterwards, he may be given a half or the whole of a plantain, well mixed with a spoon of olive oil, mixed with a spoon of lime juice. If he feels thirsty, he should be given water boiled and cooled, or the juice of lime,—never unboiled water. His clothes should be as few as possible, and should be frequently changed. Even persons suffering from typhoid and the like diseases have been completely cured by this simple treatment, and are enjoying perfect health at present. A seeming cure may also be effected by quinine, but it really brings other diseases in its train. Even in malarial fever, in which quinine is supposed to be most effective, I have rarely seen it bring permanent relief; on the other hand, I have actually seen several cases of malarial patients being permanently cured by the treatment described above.

Many people subsist on milk alone during fever, but my experience is that it really does harm in the initial stages, as it is hard to digest. If milk has to be given, it is best given in the form of "wheat-coffee", [1] or with a small quantity of rice-flour well boiled in water; but in extreme forms of fever, it ought not to be given at all. In such a condition, the juice of lime may always be given with great success. As soon as the tongue gets clean, plantain may be included in the diet, and given in the form described above. If there be constipation, a hot-water enema with borax should be applied in preference to purgatives, after which a diet of olive oil will serve to keep the bowels free.

1 Part I, chap. V

CHAPTER V
CONSTIPATION, DYSENTERY, GRIPES AND PILES

It may at first sight appear strange to have four different ailments put together in this chapter, but, as a matter of fact, they are all so closely connected, and may be cured more or less in the same way. When the stomach gets clogged by undigested matter, it leads to one or other of these diseases, according to the varying constitutions of individuals. In some it produces constipation. The bowels do not move, or move only partly, and there is great straining at stools, until it results in bleeding, or at times in the discharge of mucus, or piles. In others, it leads to diarrhea, which often ends in dysentery. In others again, it may give rise to gripes, accompanied by pain in the stomach and the discharge of mucus.

In all these cases, the patient loses his appetite, his body gets pale and weak, his tongue gets coated, and his breath foul. Many also suffer from headache and other complaints. Constipation, indeed, is so common that hundreds of pills and powders have been invented to cure it. The chief function of such patent medicines as Mother Siegel's Syrup and Eno's Fruit-salt is to relieve constipation, and hence thousands of people go in for them in the vain hope of being cured for good. Any *Vaid* or *Hakim* will tell you that constipation and the like are the result of indigestion, and that the best way to cure them is to remove the causes of indigestion; but the more candid among them will confess that they are forced to manufacture pills and powders, since the patients are not really prepared to renounce their bad habits, but at the same time want to get cured. Indeed the present-day advertisments of such medicines go to the extent of promising to those that would buy them that they need observe no directions as to diet and the like, but may eat and drink whatever they like. But my readers need not be told that this is a mere string of lies. All purgatives are invariably injurious to health. Even the mildest of them, even if they relieve the constipation, give rise to other forms of disease. If they should do any good at all, the patient should thoroughly change his ways of life, so as not to have to turn to purgatives again; otherwise, there can be no doubt that they must give rise to new diseases, even supposing that they serve to get rid of the old.

The very first thing to do in cases of constipation and the like is to reduce the quantity of food, especially such heavy things as ghee, sugar and cream of milk. Of course, he should eschew altogether wine, tobacco, bhang, tea, coffee, cocoa, and loaves made of "mill flour." The diet should consist for the most part of fresh fruits with olive oil.

The patient should be made to starve for 36 hours before treatment begins. During this time and after, mud-poultices should be applied to the abdomen during sleep; and, as has been already said, one or two "Kuhne baths" should also be taken. The patient should be made to walk for at least two hours every day. I have myself seen severe cases of constipation, dysentery, piles and gripes effectively cured by this simple treatment. Piles may not, of course, completely disappear, but they will certainly cease to give trouble. The sufferer from gripes should take special care not to take any food except lime-juice in hot water, so long as there is discharge of blood or mucus. If there is excessive griping pain in the stomach, it can be cured by warming with a bottle of hot water or a piece of well-heated brick. Needless to say, the patient should live constantly in the open air.

Fruits like the French plum, the raisin, the orange and the grape, are particularly useful in constipation. This does not, of course, mean that these fruits may be eaten even where there is no hunger. They ought not to be eaten at all in cases of gripes accompanied by a bad taste in the mouth.

CHAPTER VI
CONTAGIOUS DISEASES: SMALL-POX

Now we will proceed to deal with the treatment of contagious diseases. They have a common origin, but, since small-pox is by far the most important of them, we will give a separate chapter to it, dealing with the rest in another chapter. We are all terribly afraid of the small-pox, and have very crude notions about it. We in India even worship it as a deity. In fact it is caused, just like other diseases, by the blood getting impure owing to some disorder of the bowels; and the poison that accumulates in the system is expelled in the form of small-pox. If this view is correct, then there is absolutely no need to be afraid of small-pox. If it were really a contagious disease, everyone should catch it by merely touching the patient; but this is not always the case. Hence there is really no harm in touching the patient, provided we take some essential precautions in doing so. We cannot, of course, assert that small-pox is never transmitted by touch, for those that are physically in a condition favourable to its transmission will catch it. This is why, in a locality where small-pox has appeared, many people are found attacked by it at the same time. This has given rise to the superstition that it is a contagious disease, and hence to the attempt to mislead the people into the belief that vaccination is an effective means of preventing it. The process of vaccination consists in injecting into the skin the liquid that is obtained by applying the discharge from the body of a small-pox patient to the udder of a cow. The original theory was that a single vaccination would suffice to keep a man immune from this disease for life; but, when it was found that even vaccinated persons were attacked by the disease, a new theory came into being that the vaccination should be renewed after a certain period, and to-day it has become the rule for all persons—whether already vaccinated or not—to get themselves vaccinated whenever small-pox rages as an epidemic in any locality, so that it is no uncommon thing to come across people who have been vaccinated five or six times, or even more.

Vaccination is a barbarous practice, and it is one of the most fatal of all the delusions current in our time, not to be found even among the so-called savage races of the world. Its supporters are not content with its adoption by those who have no objection to it, but seek to impose it with the aid of penal laws and rigorous punishments on all people alike. The practice of vaccination is not very old, dating as it does only from 1798 A.D. But, during this comparatively short period that has elapsed, millions have fallen a prey to the delusion that those who get themselves vaccinated are safe from the attack of small-pox. No one can say that small-pox will necessarily attack those who have not been vaccinated; for many cases have been observed of unvaccinated people being free from its attack. From the fact that some people who are not vaccinated do get the disease, we cannot, of course, conclude that they would have been immune if only they had got themselves vaccinated.

Moreover, vaccination is a very dirty process, for the serum which is introduced into the human body includes not only that of the cow, but also of the actual small-pox patient. An average man would even vomit at the mere sight of this stuff. If the hand happens to touch it, it is always washed with soap. The mere suggestion of tasting it fills us with indignation and disgust. But how few of those who get themselves vaccinated realise that they are in effect eating this filthy stuff! Most people know that, in several diseases, medicines and liquid food are injected into the blood, and that they are assimilated into the system more rapidly than if they were taken through the mouth. The only difference, in fact, between injection and the ordinary process of eating through the mouth is that the assimilation in the former case is instantaneous, while that in the latter is slow. And yet we do not shrink from getting ourselves vaccinated! As has been well said, cowards die a living death, and our craze for vaccination is solely due to the fear of death or disfigurement by small-pox.

I cannot also help feeling that vaccination is a violation of the dictates of religion and morality. The drinking of the blood of even dead animals is looked upon with horror even by habitual meat-eaters. Yet, what is vaccination but the taking in of the poisoned blood of an innocent living animal? Better far were it for God-fearing men that they should a thousand times become the victims of small-pox and even die a terrible death than that they should be guilty of such an act of sacrilege.

Several of the most thoughtful men in England have laboriously investigated the manifold evils of vaccination, and an Anti-Vaccination Society has also been formed there. The members of this society have declared open war against vaccination, and many have even gone to gaol for this cause. Their objections to vaccination are briefly as follows:

(1) The preparation of the vaccine from the udder of cows or calves entails untold suffering on thousands of innocent creatures, and this cannot possibly be justified by any gains resulting from vaccination.

(2) Vaccination, instead of doing good, works considerable mischief by giving rise to many new diseases. Even its advocates cannot deny that, after its introduction, many new diseases have come into being.

(3) The vaccine that is prepared from the blood of a small-pox patient is likely to contain and transmit the germs of all the several diseases that he may be suffering from.

(4) There is no guarantee that small-pox will not attack the vaccinated. Dr. Jenner, the inventor of vaccination, originally supposed that perfect immunity could be secured by a single injection on a single arm; but when it was found to fail, it was asserted that vaccination on both the arms would serve the purpose; and when even this proved ineffectual, it came to be held that both the arms should be vaccinated at more than one place, and that it should also be renewed once in seven years. Finally, the period of immunity has further been reduced to three years! All this clearly shows that doctors themselves have no definite views on the matter. The truth is, as we have already said, that there is no saying that small-pox will not attack the vaccinated, or that all cases of immunity must needs be due to vaccination.

(5) The vaccine is a filthy substance, and it is foolish to expect that one kind of filth can be removed by another.

By these and similar arguments, this society has already produced a large volume of public opinion against vaccination. In a certain town, for instance, a large proportion of the people refuse to be vaccinated, and yet statistics prove that they are singularly free from disease. The fact of the matter is that it is only the self-interest of doctors that stands in the way of the abolition of this inhuman practice, for the fear of losing the large incomes that they at present derive from this source blinds them to the countless evils which it brings. There are, however, a few doctors who recognise these evils, and who are determined opponents of vaccination.

Those who are conscientious objectors to vaccination should, of course, have the courage to face all penalties or persecutions to which they may be subjected by law, and stand alone, if need be, against the whole world, in defence of their conviction. Those who object to it merely on the grounds of health should acquire a complete mastery of the subject, and should be able to convince others of the correctness of their views, and convert them into adopting those views in practice. But those who have neither definite views on the subject nor courage enough to stand up for their convictions should no doubt obey the laws of the state, and shape their conduct in deference to the opinions and practices of the world around them.

Those who object to vaccination should observe all the more strictly the laws of health already explained; for the strict observance of these laws ensures in the system those vital forces which counteract all disease germs, and is, therefore, the best protection against small-pox as well as other diseases. If, while objecting to the introduction of the poisonous vaccine into the system, they surrendered themselves to the still more fatal poison of sensuality, they would undoubtedly forfeit their right to ask the world to accept their views on the matter.

When small-pox has actually appeared, the best treatment is the "Wet-Sheet-Pack", which should be applied three times a day. It relieves the fever, and the sores heal rapidly. There is no need at all to apply oils or ointments on the sores. If possible, a mud-poultice should be applied in one or two places. The diet should consist of rice, and light fresh fruits, all rich fruits like date and almond being avoided. Normally the sores should begin to heal under the "Wet-Sheet-Pack" in less than a week; if they do not, it means that the poison in the system has not been completely expelled. Instead of looking upon small-pox as a terrible disease, we should regard it as one of Nature's best expedients for getting rid of the accumulated poison in the body, and the restoration of normal health.

After an attack of small-pox, the patient remains weak for sometime, and in some cases even suffers from other ailments. But this is due not to the small-pox itself; but to the wrong remedies employed to cure it. Thus, the use of quinine in fever often results in deafness, and even leads to the extreme form of it known as "quininism". So too, the employment of mercury in venereal diseases leads to many new forms of disease. Then again, too frequent use of purgatives in constipation brings on ailments like the piles. The only sound system of treatment is that which attempts to remove the root-causes of disease by a strict observance of the fundamental laws of health. Even the costly *Bhasmas* which are supposed to be unfailing remedies for such diseases are in effect highly injurious; for, although they may seem to do some good, they excite the evil passions, and ultimately ruin the health.

After the vesicles on the body have given place to scabs, olive oil should be constantly applied, and the patient bathed every day. Then the scabs rapidly fall off, and even the pocks soon disappear, the skin recovering its normal colour and freshness.

CHAPTER VII
OTHER CONTAGIOUS DISEASES

We do not dread chicken-pox so much as its elder sister, since it is not so fatal, and does not cause disfigurement and the like. It is, however, exactly the same as small-pox in other respects, and should therefore be dealt with in the same way.

Bubonic Plague is a terrible disease, and has accounted for the death of millions of our people since the year 1896, when it first made its real entry into our land. The doctors, in spite of all their investigations, have not yet been able to invent a sure remedy for it. Now-a-days the practice of inoculation has come into vogue, and the belief has gained ground that an attack of plague may be obviated by it. But inoculation for plague is as bad and as sinful as vaccination for small-pox. Although no sure remedy has been devised for this disease, we will venture to suggest the following treatment to those who have full faith in Providence, and who are not afraid of death.

(1) The "Wet-Sheet-Pack" should be applied as soon as the first symptoms of fever appear.

(2) A thick mud-poultice should be applied to the bubo.

(3) The patient should be completely starved.

(4) If he feels thirsty, he should be given lime-juice in cold water.

(5) He should be made to lie in the open air.

(6) There should not be more than one attendant by the side of the patient.

We can confidently assert that, if plague can be cured by any treatment at all, it can be cured by this.

Though the exact origin and causes of plague are yet unknown, it is undoubted that rats have something to do with its communication. We should, therefore, take all precautions, in a plague-infected area, to prevent the approach of rats in our dwellings; if we cannot get rid of them, we should vacate the house.

The best remedy to prevent an attack of plague is, of course, to follow strictly the laws of health,—to live in the open air, to eat plain wholesome food and in moderation, to take good exercise, to keep the house neat and clean, to avoid all evil habits, and, in short, lead a life of utter simplicity and purity. Even in normal times our lives should be such, but, in times of plague and other epidemics, we should be doubly careful.

Pneumonic Plague is an even more dangerous form of this disease. Its attack is sudden and almost invariably fatal. The patient has very high fever, feels extreme difficulty in breathing, and in most cases, is rendered unconscious. This form of plague broke out in Johannesburg in 1904, and as has been already said, 2 only one man escaped alive out of the 23 who were attacked. The treatment for this disease is just the same as that for Bubonic Plague, with this difference that the poultice should be applied in this case to both sides of the chest. If there be no time to try the "Wet-Sheet-Pack", a thin poultice of mud should be applied to the head. Needless to say, here as in other cases, prevention is better than cure.

2 Part II, chap. IV

We are terribly afraid of cholera, as of plague, but in fact, it is much less fatal. Here the "Wet-Sheet-Pack", however, is of no effect, but the mud-poultice should be applied to the stomach, and where there is a tingling sensation, the affected part should be warmed with a bottle filled with warm water. The feet should be rubbed with mustard-oil, and the patient should be starved. Care should be taken to see that he does not get alarmed. If the motions are too frequent, the patient should not be repeatedly taken out of bed, but a flat shallow vessel should be placed underneath to receive the stools. If these precautions are taken in due time, there is little fear of danger. This disease generally breaks out in the hot season, when we generally eat all sorts of unripe and over-ripe fruits in immoderate quantities and in addition to our ordinary food. The water also that we drink during this season is often dirty, as the quantity of it in wells and tanks is small, and we take no trouble to boil or filter it. Then again, the stools of the patients being allowed to lie exposed, the germs of the disease are communicated through the air. Indeed, when we consider how little heed we pay to these most elementary facts and principles, we can only wonder that we are not more often attacked by these terrible diseases.

During the prevalence of cholera, we should eat light food in moderation. We should breathe plenty of fresh air; and the water that we drink should always be thoroughly boiled, and filtered with a thick clean piece of cloth. The stools of the patient should be covered up with a thick layer of earth. Indeed, even in normal times, we should invariably cover up the stools with ashes or loose earth. If we do so, there would be much less danger of the spread of disease. Even the lower animals like the cat take this precaution, but we are worse than they in this respect.

It should also be thoroughly impressed on the minds of persons suffering from contagious diseases, as well as those around them, that they should, under no circumstances, give way to panic, for fear always paralyses the nerves and increases the danger of fatality.

CHAPTER VIII
MATERNITY AND CHILD-BIRTH

Our object in the foregoing chapters has been to point out the unity of origin and treatment of some of the more common diseases. We are, indeed, fully aware that those who are the constant victims of disease, and who are constantly oppressed by the fear of death, will still continue to put themselves at the mercy of doctors, in spite of all that we might say against it. We venture to think, however, that there would be at least a few who are willing to cure themselves of their diseases by purely natural processes, so as to save themselves from all further attacks; and such persons would surely find it worth while to follow the simple directions we have given. Before concluding this book, we will also give a few hints on maternity and the care of the child, as well as some common accidents.

In the lower orders of the animal creation, the pangs of child-birth are altogether unknown. The same should really be the case with perfectly healthy women. In fact, most women in the country regard child-birth as quite an ordinary matter; they continue to do their normal work till almost the last moment, and experience hardly any pain at the time of delivery. Women employed in labour have also been known to be able very often to return to work almost immediately after child-birth.

How comes it, then, that women in towns and cities have to endure so much pain and suffering at the time of child-birth? And why is it that they have to receive special treatment before and after the delivery?

The answer is simple and obvious. The women in towns have to lead an unnatural life. Their food, their costume, their mode of life, in general, offend against the natural laws of healthy living. Further, besides becoming pregnant at a premature age, they are the sad victims of men's lust even after pregnancy, as well as immediately after child-birth, so that conception again takes place at too short an interval. This is the state of utter misery and wretchedness in which lakhs of our young girls and women find themselves in our country to-day. To my mind, life under such conditions is little removed from the tortures of hell. So long as men continue to behave so monstrously, there can be no hope of happiness for our women. Many men put the blame on the women's shoulders; but it is none of our business here to weigh the relative guilt of man and woman in this matter. We are only concerned to recognise the existence of the evil, and to point out its cure. Let all married people realise, once for all, that, so long as sexual enjoyment at a premature age, as well as during pregnancy and soon after child-birth, does not cease to exist in our land, an easy and painless child-birth must remain a wild dream. Women silently endure the pangs of child-birth, as well as the subsequent period of confinement, under the wrong notion that they are inevitable, but they fail to see how their own ignorance and weakness of will make their children grow weaker and droop from day to day. It is the clear duty of every man and woman to try to avert this calamity at any cost. If even a single man and woman should do their duty in this matter, to that extent it would mean the elevation of the world. And this is clearly a matter in which no man need or should wait for another's example.

It follows, then, that the very first duty of the husband is wholly to abstain from all sexual intercourse with the wife from the moment of conception. And great is the responsibility that rests on the wife during the nine months that follow. She should be made to realise that the character of the child to be born will depend entirely on her life and conduct during this sacred period. If she fills her mind with love for all things that are good and noble, the child will also manifest the same disposition; if, on the other hand, she gives way to anger and other evil passions, her child will necessarily inherit the same. Hence in these nine months, she should engage herself constantly in good works, free her mind from all fear and worry, give no room for any evil thoughts or feelings, keep out all untruth from her life, and waste not a moment in idle talk or deed. The child that is born of such a mother,—how can it help being noble and strong?

The pregnant woman should, of course, keep her body as pure as her mind. She should breathe plenty of fresh air, and eat only so much of plain and wholesome food as she can easily digest. If she attends to all the directions already given in the matter of diet etc., she would have no need at all to seek the aid of doctors. If she suffers from constipation, the proportion of olive oil in the diet should be increased; and in cases of nausea or vomitting, she should take juice of lime in water without sugar. All spices and condiments should be scrupulously avoided.

The yearning for various new things that attends a woman in pregnancy may be restrained by the use of "Kuhne Baths". This is also useful in increasing her strength and vitality, and in easing the pangs of child-birth. It is also necessary to steel her mind against such yearnings by nipping in the bud each desire as it comes. The parents should be constantly mindful of the welfare of the child in the womb.

It is also the husband's duty during this period to refrain from all wranglings with his wife, and to conduct himself in such a way as to make her cheerful and happy. She should be relieved of the heavier duties of household management, and made to walk for some time every day in fresh air. And on no account should she be given any drugs or medicines during the period.

CHAPTER IX
CARE OF THE CHILD

We do not propose in this chapter to describe the duties of a midwife or wet nurse, but only to point out how the child should be cared for after birth. Those who have read the foregoing chapters need not be told how injurious it is to keep the mother during the period of confinement in a dark and ill-ventilated closet and to make her lie on a dirty bed with a fire underneath. These practices, however time-honoured they may be, are nevertheless fraught with dangerous consequences. No doubt, during the cold season, the mother should be kept warm, but this is best done by using good blankets. If the apartment is too cold and a fire has to be kept, it must be lighted outside and only brought in when all the smoke has disappeared, and even then it should not be kept under the cot on which she lies. Warmth may also be given by keeping bottles of hot water on the bed. All the clothes and sheets should be thoroughly cleansed after child-birth, and before being used again.

As the health of the child will depend entirely on that of the mother, special attention must be paid to her diet and mode of living. If she is fed on wheat, with plenty of good fruits like the plantain, and olive oil she would feel warm and strong, and have plenty of milk. Olive oil gives aperient properties to the mother's milk, and thus serves to keep the child free from constipation. If the child is unwell, attention must be turned to the state of the mother's health. Administering drugs to the child is as good as murdering it, for the child with its delicate constitution, easily succumbs to their poisonous effects. Hence the medicine should be administered to the mother, so that its beneficial properties may be transmitted to the child through her milk. If the child suffers, as it often does, from cough or loose bowels, there is no cause for alarm; we should wait for a day or so, and try to get at the root of the trouble, and then remove it. Making fuss over it and falling into a panic only makes matters worse.

The child should invariably be bathed in tepid water. Its clothing should be as little as possible; for a few months it is best to have none at all. The child should be laid on a thin soft white sheet and covered with a warm cloth. This will obviate the need for the use of shirts, prevent the clothes from getting dirty, and make the child hardy and strong. A fine piece of cloth folded into four should be placed over the navel-string, and kept in position by a band over it. The practice of tying a thread to the navel-string and hanging it round the neck is highly injurious. The navel-band should be kept loose. If the part round the navel be moist, fine well-sifted flour may be gently applied over it.

As long as the supply of the mother's milk is sufficient, the child should be fed exclusively on it; but, when it gets insufficient, fried wheat well powdered, and mixed with hot water and a little of jaggery, may be used as a substitute with quite good results. Half a plantain well mashed and mixed with half a spoonful of olive oil is also particularly beneficial. If cow's milk has to be given, it should at first be mixed with water in the proportion of three to one, and then heated until it just begins to boil, when a little of pure jaggery should also be added. The use of sugar instead of jaggery is harmful. The child should gradually be accustomed to a fruit-diet, so that its blood may be kept pure from the very beginning, and it may grow manly and bright. Those mothers who begin to feed their children on things like rice, vegetables and *dhall*, as soon as or even before its teeth have appeared, are doing them infinite harm. Needless to say, coffee and tea should be strictly eschewed.

When the child has grown big enough to walk, it may be clothed with *kurta* and the like, but its feet should still be kept bare, so that it may be free to roam about at will. The use of shoes prevents the free circulation of blood and the development of hardy feet and legs. Dressing the child in silk or lace cloths, with cap and coat, and ornaments, is a barbarous practice. Our attempt to enhance by such ridiculous means the beauty that Nature has given, only bespeaks our vanity and ignorance. We should always remember that the education of the child really begins from its very birth, and is best given by the parents themselves. The use of threats and punishments, and the practice of gorging the children with food, are an outrage on the principles of true education. As the old saying has it, "like parent, like child"; hence the example and practice of the parents necessarily shape the conduct and character of the children. If they are weaklings, their children also grow up weak and delicate; if they talk clearly and distinctly, so too will the children; but if they talk with a lisp, the children will also learn to do so. If they use foul language, or are addicted to bad habits, the children necessarily imitate them, and develop into bad characters. In fact, there is no field of human activity in which the child does not imitate the example of its parents.

We see, then, how heavy is the responsibility that rests on the shoulders of parents. The very first duty of a man is to give such education to his children as will make them honest and truthful, and an ornament to the society in which they live. In the animal and vegetable kingdoms, the offspring invariably takes after the parent. Man alone has violated this law of Nature. It is only among men that we see such incongruities as vicious children being born to virtuous parents, or sickly ones to the healthy. This is due to the fact that we thoughtlessly become parents when we are not mature enough to assume the responsibilities of that position. It is the solemn duty of all virtuous parents to train their children in noble ways. This requires that both the father and the mother should themselves have received a sound education. Where the parents lack such education and are aware of their imperfections, it is their duty to entrust their children to the care of proper guardians. It is foolish to expect that a high character can be developed in the children by merely sending them to school. Where the training given at school is inconsistent with that given at home, there can be no hope of improvement for the child.

As already pointed out, the true education of the child begins from the very moment of its birth. The rudiments of knowledge are imbibed almost in the course of play. This, indeed, was the ancient tradition; the practice of sending children to school is a growth of yesterday. If only the parents would do their duty by their children, there would be no limit to the possibilities of their advancement. But, in fact, we make playthings of our children. We deck their persons with fine clothes and jewels, we gorge them with sweetmeats, and spoil them from their very infancy by fondlings and caresses. We let them go unchecked on their way in our false affection for them. Being ourselves miserly, sensuous, dishonest, slothful and uncleanly, is it to be wondered at that our children should follow in our foot steps, and turn out weak and vicious, selfish and slothful, sensuous and immoral? Let all thoughtful parents ponder well over these matters; for on them depends the future of our land.

CHAPTER X
SOME ACCIDENTS: DROWNING

We will now turn our attention to some of the more common accidents, and the methods of dealing with them. A knowledge of these things is essential to everybody, so that timely help may be rendered, and the loss of many precious lives averted. Even children should be taught to deal with these cases, as in that way they are the more likely to grow up kind and thoughtful citizens.

And first we will deal with drowning. As man cannot live without air for more than 5 minutes at the most, little life generally remains in a drowning man taken out of water. Immediate steps should, therefore, be taken to bring him back to life. Two things have specially to be done for these,—artificial respiration, and the application of warmth. We should not forget that very often such 'First aid' has to be rendered by the side of tanks and rivers, where all the needed materials are not easily available, and such aid can be most effectual only when there are at least two or three men on the spot. The first-aider should also possess the qualities of resourcefulness, patience, and briskness; if he himself loses his presence of mind, he can do nothing. So too, if the attendants begin to discuss methods, or quarrel over details, there is no hope for the man. The best one in the party should lead, and the others should implicitly follow his directions.

As soon as the man is taken out of water, his wet clothes should be removed, and his body wiped dry. Then he should be made to lie on his face, with his hands under the head. Then, with our hand on his chest, we should remove from his mouth the water and dirt that might have got in. At this time his tongue would come out of his mouth, when it should be caught hold of with a kerchief, and held till consciousness returns. Then he should at once be turned over, with the head and the chest a little raised above the feet. Then one of the attendants should kneel by his head, and slowly spread out and straighten his arms on either side. By this means his ribs will be raised, and the air outside can enter into his body; then his hands should be quickly brought back and folded on his chest, so that the chest may contract and the air be expelled. In addition to this, hot and cold water should be taken in the hands and poured on his chest. If a fire can be lighted or procured, the man should be warmed with it. Then all the available clothes should be wrapped round his body, which should be thoroughly rubbed for warmth. All this should be tried for a long time without losing hope. In some cases, such methods have to be applied for several hours on end before breathing is restored. As soon as signs of consciousness appear, some hot drink should be administered. The juice of lime in hot water, or decoction of cloves, pepper, and the bark of the bay-tree, will be found specially effective. The smell of tobacco may also prove useful. People should not be allowed to crowd round the patient, and obstruct the free passage of air.

The signs of death in such cases are the following. The complete cessation of breathing and the beating of heart and lungs, as indicated by a piece of peacock-feather held near the nose remaining quite steady, or a mirror held near the mouth being undimmed by the moisture in the breath; the eyes remaining fixed and half-open, with heavy eye-lids; the jaws getting fixed; the fingers getting crooked; the tongue protruding between the teeth; the mouth getting frothy; nose getting red; the whole body turning pale. If all these signs simultaneously appear, we may conclude that the man is dead. In some rare cases, life may still remain even when all these signs are present. The only conclusive test of death is the setting in of decomposition. Hence the patient should never be given up for lost, until after a long and patient application of remedial measures.

CHAPTER XI
SOME ACCIDENTS—(*Contd.*)

Burns and Scalds

Very often when a man's clothes catch fire, we get into a panic, and, instead of helping the injured, make matters worse by our ignorance. It is our duty, therefore, to know exactly what to do in such cases.

The person whose clothes have caught fire should not lose his presence of mind. If the fire is only at one edge of the cloth, it should at once be squeezed out with the hands; but if it has spread over the whole cloth or a large portion of it, the man should at once lie down and roll on the floor. If a thick cloth like a carpet be available, it should at once be wrapped round his body; and if water is at hand, it should also be poured over it. As soon as the fire has been put out, we should find out if there are burns in any part of the body. The cloth would generally stick to the body where there are burns, in which case it should not be forcibly torn off, but gently snipped off with a pair of scissors, leaving the affected parts undisturbed, and taking care to see that the skin does not come off. Immediately after this, poultices of pure mud should be applied to all these places, and kept in position by bandages. This will instantly relieve the burning, and ease the patient's suffering. The poultices may as well be applied over the portions of the cloth which stick on to the body. They should be renewed as soon as they begin to get dry; there is no reason to fear the touch of cold water.

Where this sort of first aid has not been rendered, the following directions will be found very useful. Fresh plantain leaves well smeared with olive or sweet oil should be applied over the burns. If plantain leaves are not available, pieces of cloth may be used. A mixture of linseed oil and lime-water in equal proportions may also be applied with great advantage. The portions of cloth which adhere to the burns may be easily removed by moistening them with a mixture of tepid milk and water. The first bandage of oil should be removed after two days, and afterwards fresh bandages applied every day. If blisters have formed on the burnt surface, they should be pricked, but the skin need not necessarily be removed.

If the skin has simply got red by the burn, there is no more effective remedy than the application of a mud poultice. If the fingers have been burnt, care should be taken, when the poultice is applied, that they do not touch against one another. This same treatment may be applied in cases of acid-burns, and scalds of every description.

CHAPTER XII
SOME ACCIDENTS—(*Contd.*)

Snake-bite

There is no limit to the superstitions current among us in regard to snakes. From time immemorial we have cultivated a terrible fear of the snake; we even dread the very mention of its name. The Hindus worship the serpent, and have set apart a day in the year (*Nagapanchami*) for that purpose. They suppose that the earth is supported by the great serpent Sesha. God Vishnu is called *Seshasayee*, as he is supposed to sleep on the Serpent-God; and God Siva is supposed to have a garland of serpents round his neck! We say that such and such a thing cannot be described even by the thousand-tongued Adisesha, implying our belief in the snake's knowledge and discretion. The serpent Karkotaka is said to have bitten King Nala and deformed him, so that he might not suffer any harm in the course of his wanderings. Such conceptions are also to be met with among the Christian nations of the West. In English a man is very often described to be as wise and cunning as a serpent. And in the Bible, Satan is said to have assumed the shape of a serpent in order to tempt Eve.

The real reason for the popular dread of snakes is obvious. If the snake's poison should spread over the whole body, death must necessarily ensue; and since the idea of death is so dreadful to us, we dread the very name of a snake. Hence, our worship of the snake is really based on our fear. If the snake were a little creature, it would hardly be worshipped by us; but since it is a big creature, and a strangely fascinating one, it has come to be deified and worshipped.

The Western scientists of to-day hold that the snake is merely a creature of instinct, and it should be destroyed forthwith wherever found. From the official statistics, we gather that not less than 20,000 persons die every year in India of snake-bite alone. The destruction of every venomous snake is rewarded by the state, but it is really a question if the country has benefitted by it in any way. We find from experience that a snake never bites wantonly, but only as a retaliatory measure when it is molested in any way. Does this not bespeak its discretion, or at the least its innocence? The attempt to rid Hindustan, or any portion thereof, of snakes is as ridiculous and futile as trying to wrestle with the air. It may be possible to prevent snakes coming to a particular place by a systematic process of extermination, but this can never be done on a large scale. In a vast country like India, it would be an altogether foolish enterprise to try to avoid snake-bites by wholesale destruction of the snakes.

Let us never forget that the serpents have been created by the same God who created us and all other creatures. God's ways are inscrutable, but we may rest assured that He did not create animals like the lion and the tiger, the serpent and the scorpion, in order to bring about the destruction of the human race. If the serpents were to meet in council and conclude that man has been created by God for their destruction, seeing that he generally destroys a snake wherever found, should we approve of their conclusion? Surely not. In the same way, we are wrong in regarding the serpent as a natural enemy of man.

The great St. Francis of Asissi, who used to roam about the forests, was not hurt by the serpents or the wild beasts, but they even lived on terms of intimacy with him. So too, thousands of *Yogis* and *Fakirs* live in the forests of Hindustan, amidst lions and tigers and serpents, but we never hear of their meeting death at the hands of these animals. It might, however, be contended that they must certainly be meeting their death in the forests, but that we do not hear of it, as we live so far away. Granted; but we cannot deny that the number of *Yogis* that live in the forests is nothing in comparison with that of the serpents and wild beasts, so that, if these animals were really the natural enemies of man, the whole race of *Yogis* and other dwellers in the forests should become very rapidly extinct, especially since they have no weapons with which to defend themselves against their attacks. But they have by no means become extinct, and we may conclude, therefore, that they have been allowed to live unmolested in the forests by the serpents and wild beasts. In fact, I have implicit faith in the doctrine that, so long as man is not inimical to the other creatures, they will not be inimical to him. Love is the greatest of the attributes of man. Without it the worship of God would be an empty nothing. It is, in short, the root of all religion whatsoever.

Besides, why should we not regard the cruelty of the serpents and the wild beasts as merely the product and reflection of man's own nature? Are we any the less murderous than they? Are not our tongues as venomous as the serpent's fangs? Do we not prey upon our innocent brethren much in the same way as lions and leopards? All scriptures proclaim that, when man becomes absolutely harmless, all the other animals will begin to live on terms of intimacy with him. When feuds and conflicts as fierce as that between the lion and the lamb are going on within our own breasts, is it any wonder that such things should go on in the external world? For, we are but the reflection of the world around us; all the features of the external world are found reflected in the inner world of our mind. When we change our nature, the world around should also inevitably change. Do we not find that the world assumes a totally different aspect to those individual men and women who change their own nature by strenuous self-discipline? This is the great mystery of God's creation as well as the great secret of true happiness. Our happiness or otherwise rests entirely upon what we are; we have no need to depend on other people at all in this matter.

Our excuse for writing at such length on snake-bite is this. Rather than merely prescribe cure for snake-bite, we thought it as well to go a little more deeply into the matter, and point out the best way of getting rid of our foolish fears. If even a single reader were to adopt in practice the principles we have been discussing, we shall consider our effort amply rewarded. Moreover, our object in writing these pages is not merely to give the generally accepted hygienic principles, but to go to the root of the matter, and deal with the most fundamental principles of health.

Modern investigations have also shown that the man who is perfectly healthy, whose blood has not been tainted by excess of heat, and whose food is wholesome and *Satvic*, is not immediately affected by the poison of the snake, but that, on the other hand, its effect is instantaneous as well as fatal on the man whose blood has been tainted by drink or unwholesome food. One doctor goes so far as to say that the blood of the man who eschews salt and the like, and lives exclusively on a fruit-diet, remains so pure that no kind of poison can have any effect on him. I have not had enough experience myself to say how far this is true. The man whose diet has been free from salt and the like for only one or two years cannot be said to have attained this stage of perfect immunity, for the blood which has been tainted and poisoned by bad practices continued for years cannot be brought back to its normal state of purity in the short period of a year or two.

It has further been scientifically demonstrated that a man under the influence of fear or anger is much more and much sooner, affected by poison than when in the normal condition. Everybody knows how fear and anger make the pulse and the heart beat faster than the normal rate, and the quicker the flow of blood in the veins, the greater the heat generated. But the heat generated by evil passions is not healthy, but extremely harmful. Anger is, indeed, nothing but a variety of fever. Hence the best antidote against snake-bite is to use pure and *Satvic* food in moderation, to rid our minds of all evil passions like anger and fear, to refrain from giving way to panic, to retain perfect confidence in the saving power of a pure and godly life, and to remain self-possessed in the full faith that we are ever in

God's hands, and that the span of life which He has allotted to us can on no account be curtailed or exceeded.

Dr. Fitz-Seaman, the Director of the Port Elizabeth Museum, who has devoted a large portion of his life to the study of snakes, their varieties and their habits, and who is a great authority on snake-bite and its cure, has told us, as a result of his numerous experiments, that the majority of the so-called deaths by snake-bite are really caused by fear and the wrong remedies applied by quacks.

We should remember that all snakes are not venomous, and that even the bite of all venomous snakes is not immediately fatal either. Moreover, the snakes do not always get an opportunity of injecting their venom into the body of their victim. We should not, therefore, give way to panic even when we are bitten by a venomous serpent, especially since very simple remedies are available, which can be applied by ourselves without any aid from others.

The part of the body immediately above the point at which the snake has bitten should be tied round with tight bandage, which should be further strengthened by means of strong pencils or pieces of wood, so that the poison may not ascend through the veins. Then the wound should be cut half an inch deep with the fine point of a knife, so that the poisoned blood may freely flow, and the hollow should be filled with the dark-red powder sold in the bazaars and known as Potassium Permanganate. If this is not available, the blood issuing from the wound should be well sucked and spat out, by the patient himself or by somebody else, until all the poison has been removed. Of course, no man who has a wound on the lips or the tongue should be allowed to suck this poisoned blood. This treatment should be applied within 7 minutes of the accident,—that is to say, before the poison has had time to ascend and diffuse through the body. As already mentioned, the German doctor who has specialised in mud-cure, claims to have cured snake-bite by burying the patient under fresh earth. Although I have not tried the use of mud in snake-bites, I have unbounded faith in its efficacy from my experience in other cases. After the application of Potassium Permanganate (or the sucking out of the blood, in the alternative,) a poultice of mud half an inch in thickness, and big enough to cover the whole region around and above the affected part, should be applied. There should be kept in every home a quantity of well-sifted and powdered mud in a tin ready for use. It should be so kept as to be exposed to light and air, and free from dampness. Suitable bandages of cloth should also be kept so as to be within reach when needed. These will be found useful not only in snake-bite, but in numberless other cases as well.

If the patient has lost consciousness, or if respiration seems to have ceased, the process of artificial respiration already described in connection with drowning should be resorted to. Hot water, or preferably a decoction of cloves and the bark of the bay-tree, is very useful for recovering consciousness. The patient should be kept in the open air, but if his body seems to have taken cold, bottles of hot water should be employed, or a piece of flannel dipped in hot water and wrung out should be rubbed over the body, to produce warmth.

CHAPTER XIII
SOME ACCIDENTS—(*Contd.*)

Scorpion-Sting

Our familiar expression, "May God never give any man the pain of scorpion-sting", shows how keen that pain is. In fact, this pain is even sharper than that of snake-bite, but we do not dread it so much, since it is much less fatal. Indeed, as Dr. Moor has said, the man whose blood is perfectly pure has little to fear from the sting of a scorpion.

The treatment for scorpion-sting is very simple. The affected part should be cut into with a sharp-pointed knife, and the blood that issues from it slightly sucked out. A small bandage tied tightly above this portion would prevent the spread of the poison, while a poultice of mud would give immediate relief to the pain.

Some writers advise us to tie a thick bandage of cloth over the affected part, wetted with a mixture of vinegar and water in equal proportions, or to keep the region around it immersed in salt water. But the poultice of mud is certainly the most effective remedy of all, as may be personally tested by those who may have the misfortune to be stung by scorpions. The poultice should be as thick as possible; even two seers of mud would not be too much for the purpose. If the finger be stung, for instance, the poultice should extend up to the elbow. If the hand be kept immersed for sometime in wet mud in a pretty large vessel, it would give instant relief to the pain.

The stings of the centipede and other animals should be dealt with exactly as that of the scorpion.

CHAPTER XIV
CONCLUSION

I have now said all that I had intended to say on the subject of health. And now, before finally taking leave of my readers, I will say a word or two on my object in writing these pages.

One question which I have asked myself again and again, in the course of writing this book, is why I of all persons should write it. Is there any justification at all for one like me, who am no doctor, and whose knowledge of the matters dealt with in these pages must be necessarily imperfect, attempting to write a book of this kind?

My defence is this. The "science" of medicine is itself based upon imperfect knowledge, most of it being mere quackery. But this book, at any rate, has been prompted by the purest of motives. The attempt is here made not so much to show how to cure diseases as to point out the means of preventing them. And a little reflection will show that the prevention of disease is a comparatively simple matter, not requiring much specialist knowledge, although it is by no means an easy thing to put these principles into practice. Our object has been to show the unity of origin and treatment of all diseases, so that all people may learn to treat their diseases themselves when they do arise, as they often do, in spite of great care in the observance of the laws of health.

But, after all, why is good health so essential, so anxiously to be sought for? Our ordinary conduct would seem to indicate that we attach little value to health. If health is to be sought for in order that we might indulge in luxury and pleasure, or pride ourselves over our body and regard it as an end in itself, then indeed it would be far better that we should have bodies tainted with bad blood, by fat, and the like.

All religions agree in regarding the human body as an abode of God. Our body has been given to us on the understanding that we should render devoted service to God with its aid. It is our duty to keep it pure and unstained from within as well as from without, so as to render it back to the Giver, when the time comes for it, in the state of purity in which we got it. If we fulfil the terms of the contract to God's satisfaction, He will surely reward us, and make us heirs to immortality.

The bodies of all created beings have been gifted with the same senses, and the same capacity for seeing, hearing, smelling and the like; but the human body is supreme among them all, and hence we call it a "*Chintamani*," or a giver of all good. Man alone can worship God with knowledge and understanding. Where devotion to God is void of understanding, there can be no true salvation, and without salvation there can be no true happiness. The body can be of real service only when we realise it to be a temple of God and make use of it for God's worship; otherwise it is no better than a filthy vessel of bones, flesh and blood, and the air and water issuing from it are worse than poison. The things that come out of the body through the pores and other passages are so filthy that we cannot touch them or even think of them without disgust; and it requires very great effort to keep them tolerably clean. Is it not most disgraceful that, for the sake of this body, we should stoop to falsehood and deceit, licentious practices and even worse? Is it not equally shameful that, for the sake of these vices, we should be so anxious to preserve this fragile frame of ours at any cost?

This is the truth of the matter in regard to our body; for the very things which are the best or the most useful have inherent in them capabilities of a corresponding mischief. Otherwise, we should hardly be able to appreciate them at their true worth. The light of the sun, which is the source of our life, and without which we cannot live for an hour, is also capable of burning all things to ashes. So too, a king may do infinite good to his subjects, or be the source of untold mischief. Indeed, the body may be a good servant, but, when it becomes a master, its powers of evil are unlimited.

There is an incessant struggle going on within us between our Soul and Satan for the control of our body. If the soul gains the ascendancy, the body becomes a most potent instrument of good; but, if the devil is victorious in the struggle, it becomes a hot-bed of vice. Hell itself would be preferable to the body which is the slave of vice, which is constantly filled with decaying matter and which emits filthy odours, whose hands and feet are employed in unworthy deeds, whose tongue is employed in eating things that ought not to be eaten or in uttering language that ought not to be uttered, whose eyes are employed in seeing things that ought not to be seen, whose ears are employed in the hearing of things that ought not to be heard, and whose nose is employed in the smelling of things that ought not to be smelt. But, while hell is never mistaken for heaven by anybody, our body which is rendered worse than hell by ourselves is, strangely enough, regarded by us as almost heavenly! So monstrous is our vanity, and so pitiful our pride, in this matter! Those who make use of a palace as a latrine, or vice versa, must certainly reap the fruit of their folly. So too, if, while our body is really in the Devil's hands, we should fancy that we are enjoying true health, we shall have only ourselves to thank for the terrible consequences that are sure to follow.

To conclude, then our attempt in these pages has been to teach the great truth that perfect health can be attained only by living in obedience to the laws of God, and defying the power of Satan. True happiness is impossible without true health, and true health is impossible without a rigid control of the palate. All the other senses will automatically come under our control when the palate has been brought under control. And he who has conquered his senses has really conquered the whole world, and he becomes a part of God. We cannot realise Rama by reading the Ramayana, or Krishna by reading the Gita, or God by reading the Koran, or Christ by reading the Bible; the only means of realising them is by developing a pure and noble character. Character is based on virtuous action, and virtuous action is grounded on Truth. Truth, then, is the source and foundation of all things that are good and great. Hence, a fearless and unflinching pursuit of the ideal of Truth and Righteousness is the key-note of true health as of all else. And if we have succeeded (in however feeble a measure) in bringing this grand fact home to our reader, our object in writing these pages would have been amply fulfilled.